Pojanee Vatanapan's THAI COOKBOOK

Pojanee Vatanapan's THAI COOKBOOK
with Linda Alexander

HARMONY BOOKS/NEW YORK

Published by Harmony Books,
a division of Crown Publishers, Inc.,
225 Park Avenue South,
New York, New York 10003, and represented in Canada
by the Canadian MANDA Group
HARMONY and colophon are trademarks of
Crown Publishers, Inc.
Manufactured in the United States of America

Library of Congress Cataloging-in-Publication Data
Pojanee Vatanapan.
Pojanee Vatanapan's Thai cookbook.
Includes index.
1. Cookery, Thai. I. Alexander, Linda (Linda S.)
II. Title
TX724.5.T5P65   1986   641.59593   85-30510
ISBN 0-517-55968-4

10 9 8 7 6 5 4 3 2
First Edition

CONTENTS

INTRODUCTION
9

EQUIPMENT AND INGREDIENTS
13

CURRY PASTES
Nam Prik Kaeng
21

DIPPING PASTES
Nam Prik
27

SOUPS
Tom Yam Kaeng Jud Leh Soup
33

RICE
Khow
45

APPETIZERS AND SALADS
Khong Wang Leh Salut
55

CHICKEN AND DUCK
Gai Leh Pbet
71

PORK
Moo
83

BEEF
Nuea
93

SEAFOOD
Tat-Le
103

NOODLES
Kuwae Tee-Ow Leh Sen
117

DESSERTS
Kha-Nom
133

MENUS
145

SOURCE GUIDE
153

INDEX
154

Pojanee Vatanapan's
THAI
COOKBOOK

INTRODUCTION

I grew up in Damnoen Saduak, a small village located in south central Thailand. It is the site of the famous Floating Market, and every day I would see hundreds of vendors float their exotic wares on the canals in long rafts, called *thalad nam*. These buoyant peddlers would vie with one another in their loudest voices, proclaiming that they each had the best prices and the best produce. In the early morning hours, when the din was the loudest, my mother would shop for her family, cajoling, bullying and bartering until she actually did get the best prices for the best produce. For me, it was a daily adventure to assist my mother. As the youngest daughter in a family of ten, I began helping my mother with the cooking and shopping at a very early age. In Thailand it is customary for the youngest daughter to assist her mother with the cooking chores, while the oldest daughter minds the other children. Although all Thai women raised in the traditional way are taught to cook, it is the youngest daughter's daily duty. With my large family, I got a great deal of solid experience and training.

Our house was built on poles over the Lad-Pli Canal. My parents still live in their spacious teak cottage, with two of my brothers and their families. In the back of the house is a small grove with a cluster of fragrant makrud lime trees. The leaves of these trees are used for flavoring soups, and the bumpy skins of the dark green fruit are mashed into curries. My very first chore, when I was four years old, was to collect the makrud leaves and gather the different herbs that grew near our house. Then, as I became a little older and stronger, I would take the leaves and herbs I collected and grind them on the *khrok*. A khrok is an indented stone that is beaten with large, smooth rocks to crush and blend the herbs and spices. It took hours to blend

them well and even longer to satisfy my mother, who is a perfection-
ist. Today I use a mortar and pestle or my food processor.

I was an avid cooking student, and by the time I was twelve years
old I had developed quite a reputation in our village. Neighbors
frequently stopped by to sample the products of my skill. Actually, I
think a lot of my good cooking fortune had to do with my mother's
good *nam pla*, or fish sauce. Fish sauce is one of the main ingredients
in Thai cooking, and because my family lived directly on a canal with
plenty of fish, we made our own. My mother would ferment her nam
pla, using anchovies and other tiny fish, in a large clay pot with a
green dragon painted on the front. The pot was kept out in the
backyard, far away from the house. How I would dread helping my
mother as she skimmed the deep amber liquid; the smell was terri-
ble, but the taste remarkable. Today's brown, commercial version is a
pallid reminder of the nam pla I knew as a child.

In the early 1970s I lived with one of my older sisters in Bangkok
while studying to become a mathematics teacher. It was during this
period that I was exposed to the many wonderful cuisines of Thailand.

My sister had several friends who worked in the kitchens of the
large international hotels in Bangkok. They would often drop by, and
I would persuade them to show me their techniques for *chan nung*
cooking, or classical Thai cuisine. As I learned more, I began experi-
menting and integrating the chan nung techniques with the food of
the countryside I grew up with, known as *chan song*. Now that I live
in America, I have taught myself how to make even more adaptations.

Adaptation comes easily to a Thai person; it is so deeply rooted in
our culture. The people who are now called Thai adapted themselves
to a new land and new culture in the thirteenth century, and this
population was already the product of two ancient cultures, Indian
and Chinese. The original population came from the Nan Chao state
in southwestern China, located just north of the Indo-Chinese Penin-
sula. They migrated to what was then an area of the Cambodian
Empire to avoid the invading Mongolians. Through the ensuing
centuries and many wars with the Cambodians and other neighbor-
ing countries, Thailand became a sovereign nation, with its current
borders. But the people still retain the cultural accent of their
Chinese and Indian forebears.

Today's Thai population is approximately 85 percent Thai ethnic,

12 percent Chinese and 3 percent Malaysian, Cambodian and Vietnamese. All of these influences are reflected in our cuisine. For example, the Thai *kaengs* strongly resemble the curries of India—a direct influence of the original Thai ethnics. The Chinese introduced stir-fry cooking to Thai cuisine. Peanuts and fish sauce are two distinct ingredients used throughout the Southeast Asian countries. In essence, Thai cuisine is not just one type of cooking, but an amalgamation of many, resulting from diverse cultures and historical circumstances.

My family is part Chinese, as are most of the people who settled in Damnoen Saduak. Several recipes in this cookbook are my mother's Thai versions of familiar Chinese dishes. Other dishes, both classical and provincial, I learned when I lived in Bangkok. The basic measurements given in this book are to be used as guidelines. Thai cooking is a taste-and-season cuisine, a tradition handed down from mother to daughter, rarely written down as recipes.

In 1978 I met my husband-to-be, George Bilinsky, while he was on vacation in Thailand. Within four years, we had married, moved to New York and opened our first restaurant. I love my new country, and New York offers so much variety in terms of cuisine. Still, I find myself constantly seeking out new ways of adapting the dishes of my homeland to the available ingredients here in the States. I also have to keep in mind the different natures of the palate when preparing meals for American guests. I use many of the more fiery spices sparingly, as indicated in my recipes.

Preparing and Serving the Thai Meal

A typical Thai dinner for four to six people includes a large bowl of rice, one or two soups, a non-spicy stir-fried vegetable dish, a curry dish (kaeng) and a *pad,* which is a spicy meat or fish dish. A plate of fresh raw vegetables is also served with *nam prik,* or pepper condiment, on the side.

This may seem like a lot of work and a lot of food, but this is how Thais eat every night. Because we never worry about serving the various dishes uniformly heated and much of the preparation is done in advance, it's really quite easy. The key is to have a few basics on hand, such as fish sauce, rice, coconut milk and red curry paste, homemade or canned, and to have all the ingredients cut up and ready to cook. With a little practice you can have a traditional Thai meal on the table in less than an hour.

Start with a curry paste. Once prepared, it will keep in the refrigerator for two months. Next, begin steaming the rice on a back burner or in a rice steamer and move on to the preparation of the kaeng, which involves mixing the curry paste into coconut milk and simmering these ingredients with vegetables and beef, fish or chicken.

Once the curry dish is cooked, set it aside, in the pot, near the heat until ready to serve. Then start the soups, which are usually made from the same base, either chicken stock or black soy sauce. While the soups simmer, chop the ingredients for the pad and the cooked vegetable dish. Both of them are stir-fried and cook in minutes.

Finally, make the nam prik in one step by mashing the ingredients with a mortar and pestle or in a food processor. Nam prik can also be prepared in advance and refrigerated for up to two weeks.

It is customary to eat a Thai meal with a large spoon for mixing the different dishes with rice. A fork is used to hold the food stationary while the spoon cuts or scoops. Chopsticks are used only with noodle dishes, although in some rural areas farmers eat with chopsticks exclusively.

At the table, each person is served a heaping plate of rice, covering the entire dish. Then bite-size pieces are spooned from the various platters of food, to be mixed in with the rice; it is not proper to scoop out large portions at any one time. Everyone serves themselves. The soups are sipped from communal bowls, placed strategically in the center of the table. In Thailand, soups are consumed as beverages, not as a first course.

A Thai meal is like a community get-together. Maybe that's because of our community-sized families. Still, there is a special kind of feeling when eating Thai style. There's the warmth of spirit because you are really sharing the food. In fact, before the meal begins we say *rap-pra-taarn:* sit down to share this food.

EQUIPMENT AND INGREDIENTS

Thai cuisine uses many ingredients that are found only in Thailand, especially vegetables and fruits. This book contains recipes that use ingredients easily found in this country, or easily substituted. Fortunately, there are Oriental markets in almost every major city, as well as an abundance of mail-order suppliers. Check the Source Guide on page 153. Spanish markets and health food stores are also good sources.

Equipment

WOK The wok is a bowl-shaped frying pan that is excellent for quick stir-frying. The shape allows for maximum heat distribution without burning. If you intend to do a lot of Thai cooking, it is an excellent investment, as it is much easier to use than a frying pan for stir-fry dishes.

I prefer a wok made out of steel, which is the traditional material used in Oriental woks. It should be at least 14 inches in diameter, to hold all of your ingredients. Before using a steel wok for the first time you must season it. Scrub it inside and outside with steel wool to remove the protective coating used in shipping, then spread a couple of tablespoons of vegetable oil on the inside, letting the excess oil drip into the center. Slowly heat the wok until the oil begins to smoke, remove it from the heat and let it cool. With a paper towel or cloth wipe off the remaining oil, leaving only a thin coat. Always leave a little oil on the inner surface of the wok to prevent rusting.

Two other utensils are always used with a wok and should be purchased at the same time. One is a ring to sit the wok on over the burner, and the other is a cover or lid. Quite often woks are sold with these items, but be sure to check.

Khrok A *khrok* is a flat stone with an indentation that is used like a mortar and pestle for grinding dry ingredients. The khrok and mortar and pestle are the traditional Thai ways to grind herbs and spices, but a food processor or a good blender can be just as effective.

STEAMER Many Thai dishes, such as the Tapioca Balls on page 60, are prepared by steam cooking. This method cooks the food by circulating the steam from boiling water. There is virtually no oil used in this type of preparation, and it is very healthy, allowing the foods to retain their minerals and vitamins, as well as keeping them moist and delicious. There are several utensils available for steam cooking. The traditional steamer is made out of bamboo and perches inside the wok. Another type of steamer is a stainless-steel basket (often called a vegetable steamer) that fits into almost any pot or pan. The flat steam trays can be bought in various sizes and are designed to fit on the rim of a pot or pan. I use a steel-and-aluminum pot that has a removable basket for steaming, called a steam pot.

Basic Ingredients

BEAN CURD *(Thao Hu)*   Also known as tofu or bean cake, bean curd is a white cake made from soybeans. Low in calories and an excellent source of protein, it is eaten at breakfast in soups, or sauteed with noodles and vegetables. Buy the firm variety of bean curd, because it is easier to cut and cook with. It can be found in Oriental markets, health food stores and many supermarkets. Bean curd will keep in the refrigerator for two weeks if the water is changed daily.

CHINESE CABBAGE *(Bok Choy)*   Bok choy is used in much of Thai cooking. It has a long white stem topped with dark green leaves. It is usually prepared by sauteing.

COCONUT MILK *(Ka-ti)*   Coconut milk is prepared from the flesh of the coconut, not the water from the middle of the seed. It is the main ingredient in most curries. If you use canned coconut milk, make sure you buy the unsweetened kind. To make your own, remove the white coconut meat from the shell with a nutpick and grate it into a bowl, or buy dried, shredded, unsweetened coconut meat (desiccated). Combine equal amounts of coconut meat and boiling water in a bowl and let the mixture steep for at least two hours. Strain the liquid through two layers of fine cheesecloth. Coconut milk will keep in the refrigerator for one week.

PALM SUGAR *(Nam Thaan Bip)*   Palm sugar is made from the sap of the palm tree, in a process similar to maple sugaring. It is a dark, thick sugar with a honey-like texture, usually sold in jars. If it is unavailable in your area, substitute light brown sugar.

PEANUTS *(Tua)*   Peanuts are frequently used in Thai dishes, in many forms: crushed, whole and ground. Buy unsalted peanuts for cooking, because there is plenty of salt in the sauces.

PICKLED TURNIPS *(Hua Chai Po)* Pickled turnips are usually found in jars or plastic-wrapped refrigerator bags, depending on whether you use Thai, Chinese or Japanese versions. All types are good, and the differences are subtle. In Thai cooking pickled turnips are chopped and cooked with noodles and meats.

RICE *(Khow)* The word for rice in the Thai language, *khow*, also means food, because rice is the focal point of a meal. In Thailand, polished, long-grain white rice is prepared by steaming (see page 46).

SHRIMP PASTE *((Kapi)* Shrimp paste is made from tiny dried shrimp and chili peppers, crushed together. It has a very pungent smell and taste. Thais love it and use it as the base for the nam priks, or pepper condiments, that are served at every meal. If you cannot find shrimp paste, substitute anchovy paste, but use half the amount called for in the recipe.

STICKY RICE *(Khow Neeow)* Also known as sweet rice and glutinous rice, sticky rice is a short-grain variety used in desserts, usually mixed with coconut milk. It can be purchased at Oriental food markets.

STRAW MUSHROOMS *(Hed)* Used in various curries and soups, straw mushrooms are available in this country in cans. They are never sliced or chopped, only used whole, and can be replaced by regular canned mushrooms, if necessary.

TAMARIND *(Ma Kham)* Tamarind pods, used in Thai curries, grow in Southeast Asia, India and South America. The pulp is dark brown and very sour, but when it is soaked in water and strained it has a distinct tangy flavor. Tamarind pods can sometimes be found fresh, but are usually sold dried or frozen. Spanish markets carry a bottled tamarind syrup that is quite good. If you use this syrup, reduce or omit the sugar called for in most recipes. If you cannot find tamarind in any form, substitute a mixture of half lemon juice and half water equal to the amount called for in the recipe.

TAPIOCA *(Saku)* Tapioca is used in various desserts and appetizers, but most frequently when making tapioca balls. For Thai cooking use the "small pearl" variety available in most supermarkets.

VEGETABLE OIL *(Nam-Man Put)* Thai cooking includes a great deal of stir-frying. I suggest using the lightest oil available, such as vegetable oil, but peanut oil, corn oil and safflower oil are fine too.

Sauces

Sauces are used as flavorings in Thai dishes, and sometimes they are the actual bases for a gravy or soup. All of the sauces listed can be purchased in Oriental groceries, and some can even be found in supermarkets. All of these sauces, if refrigerated when opened, will keep for months.

BLACK BEAN SAUCE *(Tow Tchiow)* Black bean sauce, made from marinated whole black beans, water and salt, is used as a flavoring for vegetables. Available in cans and jars, it will keep indefinitely in the refrigerator.

BLACK SOY SAUCE *(See U Dam)* Black soy sauce is an extra-thick, dark sauce made from soybeans, starch and molasses. It is used as a base for soups and sauces, as well as a flavoring for stir-fried dishes.

FISH SAUCE *(Nam Pla)* Nam pla is the essence of Thai cooking and much of Southeast Asian cuisine in general. There are very few dishes that don't use this distinct sauce. It is sold in plastic and glass bottles, and when you first open the top you are immediately greeted with a very strong, fishy aroma. Do not be put off by its smell. The way it blends into the dishes dispels any misgivings you might have had from first whiff. Fish sauce is made from fermented anchovies, small fish and salt. In Thailand people make their own in large clay pots.

LIGHT SOY SAUCE *(See U Kow)* This is the type of soy sauce usually served in Chinese restaurants. It is sometimes used in stir-fried dishes, but is not that common in Thai cuisine.

OYSTER SAUCE *(Nam Man Hoi)* Dark, thick and sweet, oyster sauce is made from ground, dried oysters and small fish soaked in their own brine, with soy sauce and sugar. It is used in stir-fried dishes with meat, chicken or fish.

Noodles *(Sen)*

BEAN THREADS *(Woon Sen)* Woon sen noodles, also known as sai fun and cellophane noodles, are made from mung bean starch and when cooked are clear and chewy in texture. They are used in soups or stir-fried with vegetables and eggs.

RICE FLAKES *(Sen Kuwae Chap)* Rice flakes are ¼-inch-square white chips made from rice starch, and usually packaged in one-pound bags. They are used in soups or stir-fried with strong-flavored sauces.

RICE NOODLES *(Sen Lek)* These dried noodles look like white fettuccine—long and flat. They are available in one-pound bags and are used in main-course noodle dishes like Pad Thai (Sauteed Rice Noodles).

RICE VERMICELLI *(Sen Mee)* Also known as rice sticks and mai fun, rice vermicelli comes packaged in bunches of three. For deep-frying, the bunches are separated and directly placed in the oil. For stir-frying, they are soaked in water first.

Herbs and Spices

CHILI PEPPERS *(Prik)* Thai food has three distinct characteristics: sweet, salty and spicy. It is spicy because of the chili peppers. Most frequently used are the *prik chee fa,* in this country known as serrano peppers. They are about 2 inches long, very narrow and glossy, and are sold in three colors: green, red and yellow. The red ones are hotter than the green, and the yellow even hotter than the red. There is another chili pepper that can be substituted in many dishes and is sold throughout the Southwest, known as the jalapeño pepper. It is best to use fresh chili peppers, unless a recipe specifies dried.

The pods are usually sliced diagonally, very thin (⅛ to ¹/₁₆ inch), and the seeds, which are the most fiery part, are often removed. When handling chili peppers, remember to wear rubber gloves or keep your hands away from your eyes and wash them thoroughly with cold water afterward.

Two other chili peppers we use are *prik khi nu* and *prik pong*. Prik khi nu are approximately ½ inch long, very shiny and dark green or red. In this country they are called bird's-eye chilies. Spicier than prik chee fa, they are used only in Nam Pla Prik Pboen, pepper condiment. Cayenne pepper, *prik keeno,* can be used as a substitute for prik khi nu.

Prik pong are large, light green chilies. They are excellent for sauteing and are very sweet, not spicy. The closest I've seen to prik pong are the Italian frying peppers. Use them in your pad if spicy chilies are not desired.

CORIANDER *(Pak Chee)* Also called cilantro or Chinese parsley. The seeds are ground into curry pastes, the leaves are used as garnish and the aromatic stalks are sauteed in pads. My mother's secret to the success of many of her dishes was to use the roots as well as the stalks and seeds.

CRUSHED RED PEPPER *(Prik Pboen)* Crushed red pepper is really dried crushed chilies. Any commercial brand is fine to use.

CURRY POWDER *(Pong Kha-li)* A powdered blend of various spices, usually chili pepper, coriander, cumin, fennel and turmeric, it is available commercially in jars and cans, sold as curry powder. Curry powder is not to be confused with curry pastes, which are specific blends of spices used in special gravy dishes (page 21).

FIVE-SPICE POWDER *(Pong Pa-Lo)* A powder made out of several spices, with anise and cinnamon predominating. It can be bought premixed at Oriental groceries or in many supermarkets, or you can prepare your own. To make approximately 1 ounce, using a mortar and pestle or a food processor, grind together to a fine powder the following spices: 6 star anise, 2 teaspoons ground cinnamon, 15 whole cloves, ½ teaspoon fennel seeds and 1 teaspoon Szechwan peppercorns (if unavailable, use black peppercorns).

GALANGA ROOT *(Kha)* Galanga root is a rhizome, in the same family as ginger, and grows mainly in Southeast Asia. It is very difficult to find fresh galanga root in this country, so Thai cooks here usually use the dried kind. Dried kha comes in flat, round disks or powdered. When using kha disks, soak them in water until they are soft. If kha is to be used in a soup you do not have to presoak it.

GARLIC *(Kra Thiam)* There is a little garlic in almost all Thai dishes—with the exception of desserts, of course. It is a very important spice, valued for its medicinal properties and as an effective preservative for foods. Use only fresh garlic cloves, no powders. Thais eat garlic as a pickle, too. It is called *kra thiam dong*, garlic pickled with vinegar and sugar. It is absolutely delicious with rice soup.

GINGER *(Khing)* Fresh gingerroot can be peeled, sliced and soaked in water and will keep in the refrigerator for two weeks. In Thai cooking use only fresh ginger—never ginger powder.

LEMON GRASS *(Ta Krai)* This tall grass is grown mainly in the Orient and, despite the name, has no relation to the lemon tree or fruit. Some Oriental groceries import fresh lemon grass, but generally it is sold dried. If you do manage to find fresh lemon grass, be sure to try it in a salad.

MACE *(Dat Chan Taet)* Mace is the dried outer covering of the nutmeg seed. The tastes are similar, but mace is more delicate.

MAKRUD LIME *(Bai Makrud)* The makrud trees that bloom behind my parents' house in Damnoen Saduak yield the most beautiful citrus fragrance all year round. My first chore when I was a very small child was to collect the leaves and fruit of this tree. The dark green, bumpy skin of the lime is chopped into curry pastes. The leaves add their strong, tart aroma to soups, sauces and curries. And the juice, which is very similar to lemon juice, is used for cooking. Makrud lime is very difficult to buy in this country, so I use dried makrud leaves that are imported from Thailand, and substitute lemon juice and lemon zest. The zest is the yellow part of the rind only, not the bitter white pith.

ORIENTAL BASIL *(Bai Kra Prow)* The leaves are small, dark green and rough in texture, similar to fresh mint, which can be substituted. Oriental basil should not be confused with sweet basil, because they have very different tastes.

CURRY PASTES
Nam Prik Kaeng

A staple dish in the Thai culinary repertoire is the kaeng, or gravy dish. This dish is usually made with meat or fish, vegetables, coconut milk and a base that is a blend of many herbs and spices. This base is called a curry paste, nam prik kaeng, *and the texture is thick and stiff, almost like peanut butter. Many Thai women living in this country rely on canned curry pastes and doctor them up with other ingredients. Curry pastes are also packaged dry in envelopes, with instructions on how to mix them into pastes. Of course, it is worth it to take the time and make your own. Both homemade and canned Nam Prik Kaeng will keep in the refrigerator for a month if stored in a tightly covered container.*

RED CURRY PASTE
Nam Prik Kaeng Dang

The most versatile type of curry paste, it is not only used to make a delicious kaeng but is an important ingredient in peanut dressing, sate and many other dishes.

Approximately ½ cup

5 or 6 dried red chili peppers
1 stem fresh lemon grass or 1 teaspoon dried lemon grass
5 garlic cloves, peeled
3 medium shallots, peeled
1 teaspoon chopped makrud peel or lemon zest
1 teaspoon galanga root, fresh or dried (if using dried, soak in cold
    water for 15 minutes, then drain before using)

Cut the chili peppers into small pieces and soak them in a cup of cold water for 15 minutes to soften. Separate the seeds and discard them.

   Place the cut chili peppers in a mortar or food processor. Add the remaining ingredients and blend well until a thick paste, like peanut butter, is formed. If the ingredients are too dry, add a few drops of cold water. Put the curry paste in a tightly covered container in the refrigerator until ready to use.

MASAMAN CURRY PASTE
Nam Prik Kaeng Masaman

Masaman curry paste is used in meat and chicken dishes with pota-toes, so it becomes a very thick and hearty kaeng. The aroma is reminiscent of many Indian curries, and is also very spicy.

Approximately ½ cup

5 or 6 dried red chili peppers
5 garlic cloves, unpeeled
3 medium shallots, unpeeled
1½ teaspoons coriander seeds
½ teaspoon cardamom seeds
½ teaspoon ground mace
⅛ teaspoon fennel seeds
6 whole black peppercorns
1 teaspoon galanga root, fresh, dried or powdered (if using dried or
    fresh galanga, break into small pieces)
1 stem fresh lemon grass or 1 teaspoon dried lemon grass

Preheat the broiler. Cut the chili peppers into small pieces and soak them in a cup of cold water for 15 minutes. Remove the seeds and discard them. Put the garlic and shallots on a flat baking sheet and broil for 5 minutes. Allow the garlic and shallots to cool, then peel and set aside.

In a dry skillet, toast the coriander seeds, cardamom seeds, mace, fennel seeds and peppercorns over a very low flame for 5 minutes. Set aside.

In the same skillet, toast the galanga, lemon grass and chili peppers over a very low flame for 5 minutes, or until the mixture starts to brown. Put all of the ingredients in a mortar or food processor and blend until a thick paste has formed. Add drops of cold water if the mixture is too thick. Store the curry paste in a tightly covered container in the refrigerator.

PANANG CURRY PASTE
Nam Prik Kaeng Panang

Panang curry is delicious with chicken, beef, pork, liver or fish.

Approximately ½ cup

5 or 6 dried red chili peppers
¼ teaspoon fennel seeds
1 teaspoon coriander seeds
¼ teaspoon mace
1 stalk fresh lemon grass or 1 teaspoon dried lemon grass
1 teaspoon chopped makrud peel or lemon zest
1 teaspoon galanga root, fresh, dried or powdered (if using dried
    galanga, soak in cold water for 15 minutes to soften)
3 medium shallots, peeled and chopped
4 or 5 garlic cloves, peeled and chopped

Cut the chili peppers into small pieces and soak in cold water for 15 minutes. Separate the seeds and discard them. In a dry skillet, toast the fennel seeds, coriander seeds and mace over a very low flame for 5 minutes.

Put all of the ingredients in a mortar or food processor and blend to a thick red-brown paste, adding drops of cold water to get the right consistency. Store in a tightly covered container in the refrigerator until ready to use.

SOUR CURRY PASTE
Nam Prik Kaeng Sum

Sour curry paste is used in seafood and fish dishes and with sauteed vegetables. Usually made with shrimp paste, it is very pungent in both taste and aroma.

Approximately ¼ cup

5 or 6 dried red chili peppers
1½ teaspoons shrimp paste or ½ teaspoon anchovy paste
4 garlic cloves, peeled and chopped
3 medium shallots, peeled and chopped

Cut the chili peppers into small pieces and soak them in cold water for 15 minutes. Separate and discard the seeds. Put all of the ingredients in a mortar or food processor and blend until a thick, dark brown paste is formed. Add drops of cold water to maintain a thick paste consistency. Store in a tightly covered container in the refrigerator until ready to use.

GREEN CURRY PASTE
Nam Prik Kaeng Kheu Wan

Green curry paste is used in chicken and beef dishes.

Approximately ½ cup

5 or 6 fresh green chili peppers or one 4-ounce can, drained
2 stalks fresh lemon grass or 2 teaspoons dried lemon grass
5 garlic cloves, peeled and chopped
3 medium shallots, peeled and chopped
1 teaspoon chopped makrud peel or lemon zest
1 teaspoon galanga root, fresh, dried or powdered (if using dried
    galanga, soak in cold water for 15 minutes to soften)

Slice the chili peppers in half lengthwise. Discard the seeds and chop the chili peppers. Put all of the ingredients in a mortar or food processor and blend to a thick green paste, adding drops of cold water if necessary. Store in a tightly covered container in the refrigerator until ready to use.

YELLOW CURRY PASTE
Nam Prik Kaeng Khali

This extremely aromatic curry is particularly delicious when cooked with chicken, onions and potatoes.

Approximately ½ cup

5 or 6 dried red chili peppers
1 teaspoon galanga root, fresh, dried or powdered (if using dried
      galanga, soak in cold water for 15 minutes to soften)
1 stalk fresh lemon grass or 1 teaspoon dried lemon grass
3 medium shallots, peeled and chopped
3 or 4 garlic cloves, peeled and chopped
1 teaspoon coriander seeds
1 teaspoon curry powder (any commercial variety)
¼ teaspoon mace
¼ teaspoon cardamom seeds
¼ teaspoon ground cloves

Cut the dried chili peppers into small pieces and soak them in cold water for 15 minutes. Separate and discard the seeds. In a skillet, toast the remaining ingredients over a very low flame for 5 minutes.

   Put the chili peppers and the toasted spices in a mortar or food processor and blend to a thick yellow-brown paste, adding drops of cold water to get the right peanut butter-like consistency. Store in a tightly covered container in the refrigerator until ready to use.

DIPPING PASTES
Nam Prik

Nam prik *translated literally means "pepper water," but the name describes condiments or vegetable dips that are eaten with raw or steamed vegetables. They are served in place of salads at meals. The vegetables are arranged on a large platter, and a small bowl of nam prik is placed either on or adjacent to the platter.*

Most nam prik are made with kapi, or shrimp paste, but if kapi is not available, anchovy paste can be substituted; use half the amount called for in the recipe. Nam prik can be prepared a couple of days in advance, though it is never stored for any length of time because the longer it sits, even in the refrigerator, the stronger the aroma becomes.

SHRIMP PASTE SAUCE
Nam Prik Kapi

Serve with sliced cucumbers, raw string beans, celery hearts and curly or romaine lettuce.

¼ cup

1 tablespoon shrimp paste
3 garlic cloves, peeled and chopped
3 green chili peppers, seeds removed
2 tablespoons lemon juice
¼ teaspoon sugar
½ teaspoon fish sauce

With a mortar and pestle, or in a food processor, thoroughly blend the shrimp paste and garlic until thick and pasty. Add the chili peppers, lemon juice and sugar and blend until it is once again thick and pasty. When ready to serve, stir in the fish sauce.

SHRIMP AND SHRIMP PASTE SAUCE
Nam Prik Kung

Steamed and chilled cabbage and raw string beans, sliced cucumbers and celery hearts are served with this one.

Approximately ½ cup

½ pound fresh shrimp, peeled, deveined and cooked
1 tablespoon shrimp paste
2 garlic cloves, peeled and chopped
3 fresh red chili peppers, seeds removed
¼ teaspoon sugar
2 tablespoons lemon juice
½ teaspoon fish sauce

With a mortar and pestle, or in a food processor, thoroughly mash the shrimp into the shrimp paste until a smooth dark red-brown paste has formed. Add the garlic, chili peppers, sugar and lemon juice and continue blending until smooth. When ready to serve, stir in the fish sauce.

GREEN MANGO AND SHRIMP PASTE SAUCE
Nam Prik Ma Muang

This nam prik is traditionally served with raw string beans, raw zucchini squash, cucumbers, curly or romaine lettuce, fried eggplant and chilled steamed celery cabbage.

Approximately 1 cup

½ cup green mango (unripe), chopped
1 tablespoon shrimp paste
2 garlic cloves, peeled and chopped
3 fresh red chili peppers, seeds removed
1½ tablespoons lemon juice
¼ teaspoon sugar
½ teaspoon fish sauce

With a mortar and pestle, or in a food processor, thoroughly blend the mango and shrimp paste to a smooth consistency. Add the garlic, chili peppers, lemon juice, sugar and 2 tablespoons of hot water and blend to make a smooth paste. When ready to serve, stir in the fish sauce.

DRIED SHRIMP AND SHRIMP PASTE SAUCE
Nam Prik Phao

This unique sauce also doubles as a spicy seasoning in several dishes. It can be added to hot water to form a delicious broth or used in dishes such as Beef Salad (page 100). For dipping, use cucumbers, raw string beans, zucchini and curly or romaine lettuce.

Approximately ½ cup

6 medium shallots, peeled
8 to 10 garlic cloves, peeled
8 dried red chili peppers
1½ tablespoons shrimp paste
2 tablespoons vegetable oil
2 tablespoons dried shrimp, crushed
1½ tablespoons sugar
½ teaspoon fish sauce

Preheat the broiler. In a shallow baking dish, arrange the shallots, garlic and chili peppers in one layer and toast under the broiler for 7 minutes. Combine them in a bowl with the shrimp paste. Mix well. In a skillet, heat the oil until it sizzles and add the shrimp paste mixture. Cook for 3 minutes. Add the dried shrimp, sugar, fish sauce and 1 tablespoon of water. Continue cooking over a low flame for 5 minutes, or until a thick, wet paste forms. Serve warm or chilled.

GREEN CHILI PEPPERS IN FISH SAUCE
Nam Pla Prik Pboen

A nice alternative to a shrimp paste–based sauce, this sauce is used as a condiment added to rice, soups and curries for extra zip. Remember, wash your hands well after handling the chili peppers; the oils will cause severe stinging if you touch your eyes.

*   With this sauce serve lettuce, sliced cucumbers, zucchini, raw or blanched string beans and celery hearts.*

Approximately ½ cup

8 to 10 fresh green bird's-eye chili peppers
3 tablespoons lemon juice
1 tablespoon fish sauce
2 medium shallots, minced

Preheat the broiler. In a flat baking dish, layer the chili peppers so they do not overlap. Place under the broiler for 3 minutes. Allow to cool. Slice the chili peppers across diagonally. In a small ceramic or glass bowl, mix the lemon juice, fish sauce and shallots. Stir in the chili peppers and serve. This sauce will store indefinitely if refrigerated, but beware—the longer it sits, the hotter it becomes.

SOUPS
Tom Yam Kaeng
Jud Leh Soup

There are three ways of saying soup in Thai: tom yam, *for spicy soups;* kaeng jud, *for light broths; and* soup, *for soups in general. There are so many names to describe them because there are so many different types, depending upon which meal the soup is served with. Often more than one soup is served at a meal, because it is used as a beverage and served as a part of the main course.*

At a family meal, large serving bowls are placed on the table. Then everyone dips a spoon into the bowls to sip, maybe spooning out a vegetable or piece of fish and mixing it into his or her own plate of rice. If serving soup this way doesn't appeal to you, put it in a large pot or tureen and let your guests serve themselves in small bowls.

Since so many Thai soups use a light chicken broth as the base, I have included a recipe that makes enough to use in two different soups. If you plan to serve only one soup rather than two, Thai style, freeze half of the broth until you need it.

THAI CHICKEN BROTH
Soup Gai

Thai chicken broth is lighter than the Western version because it is used as a base for soups. It should never have a distinct character that might overpower the delicate herbs and spices you will be adding.

My recipe is a real country girl's—we use only the bones to make the broth, and use the meat in curries. This broth will keep in the refrigerator for two weeks or in the freezer for several months.

Makes 10 cups

Chicken bones from 2 whole chicken breasts (save the meat for
    another dish)
2 celery stalks, sliced into ½-inch pieces
1 large carrot, sliced into ½-inch rounds
1 medium onion, quartered

In a large pot, bring 11 cups of cold water to a boil. Add all of the ingredients and return to a boil for 15 minutes. Cover the pot, reduce the heat and continue simmering for 30 minutes. Strain the broth, discarding the bones and vegetables.

SPICY COCONUT MILK AND CHICKEN SOUP
Tom Kha Gai

Tom Kha Gai is a rich, tangy soup, spicy and slightly sweet. It is pale yellow, almost ivory in color. In the countryside, Tom Kha Gai is served as a snack or at dinner. It is especially good when served with a glass of mekong, the Thai version of Scotch. I have made this soup since I was very young, but when I cooked it as a child I would start from scratch—a chicken scratching in our backyard.

4 to 6 servings

5 cups Thai Chicken Broth (page 34) or chicken stock
2 cups unsweetened coconut milk (page 15)
½ cup lemon juice
½ cup fish sauce
3 or 4 pieces dried galanga root
3 or 4 lemon leaves or 1 teaspoon grated lemon zest
2 stalks finely minced lemon grass or 2 teaspoons dried lemon grass
One 8-ounce can straw mushrooms
2 whole chicken breasts, skinned, boned and sliced into 1-inch pieces
2 fresh green chili peppers, diagonally sliced ⅛-inch thick
½ teaspoon sugar

Heat the chicken broth in a large pot. Add the coconut milk and stir vigorously until blended. Add the lemon juice and fish sauce. Stir in the galanga root, lemon leaves, lemon grass, straw mushrooms and chicken. Simmer for 15 to 20 minutes, or until the chicken meat is just cooked. Stir in the chili peppers and sugar and serve hot.

ASPARAGUS SOUP WITH CRABMEAT
Soup Naw Mai

Thai soups often combine one vegetable with fish or seafood in a light broth. These soups are prepared very quickly, so the fish remains solid and the vegetables crisp. In Thailand, Soup Naw Mai is often eaten at lunch, mixed with pig's blood as a nutritious thickener, but I use arrowroot to thicken the broth slightly.

4 to 6 servings

5 cups Thai Chicken Broth (page 34) or chicken stock
½ pound asparagus, fresh or frozen, cut into ½-inch pieces
½ cup fish sauce
1 teaspoon ground black pepper
1 teaspoon sugar
½ cup crabmeat (if frozen, thaw first)
1 tablespoon arrowroot powder

Bring the chicken broth to a simmer. Add the asparagus, fish sauce, pepper and sugar.

Tear the crabmeat into bite-size pieces and add to the simmering broth.

Dissolve the arrowroot in 1 tablespoon of the broth and stir it into the soup. Continue stirring the soup for another 3 to 5 minutes, or until it has thickened slightly.

SPICY SHRIMP SOUP
Tom Yam Kung

My friend Noi likes this soup so spicy it makes my eyes water to smell it. I prefer it mildly spicy and suggest that you experiment with the crushed red pepper and add the green chili peppers at the end, when you are ready to serve.

4 to 6 servings

5 cups Thai Chicken Broth (page 34) or chicken stock
½ cup fish sauce
3 or 4 lemon leaves or 1 teaspoon grated lemon zest
4 stalks fresh lemon grass, chopped, or 1 tablespoon dried lemon
    grass
½ teaspoon sugar
One 8-ounce can straw mushrooms, drained
1 pound medium shrimp, shelled and deveined
¼ teaspoon crushed red pepper
2 green chili peppers, seeds removed and finely chopped

Bring the chicken broth to a boil and add the fish sauce, lemon leaves, lemon grass and sugar. Reduce the heat and simmer for 15 minutes. Add the mushrooms and shrimp. Continue simmering for 3 to 5 minutes, or just until the shrimp turn pink. Stir in the crushed red pepper, top with green chili peppers and serve.

OMELETTE SOUP
Kaeng Jud Kai

We eat this soup almost every night with dinner. It goes well with spicy curries.

4 to 6 servings

5 cups Thai Chicken Broth (page 34) or chicken stock
2 tablespoons vegetable oil
6 eggs, slightly beaten
¼ teaspoon ground black pepper
2 scallions, chopped
2 coriander stems with roots, finely chopped
½ cup fish sauce

In a medium-size pot, bring the chicken broth to a simmer. In a frying pan, heat the oil and add the eggs, pepper, scallions and coriander stems. When the omelette sets, turn it over and lightly brown the other side. Let the omelette cool slightly, and with your hands tear it into bite-size chunks. Add the chunks to the simmering broth. Stir in the fish sauce, simmer for another 3 minutes and serve.

BEAN CURD SOUP WITH GROUND PORK
Kaeng Jud Thao Hu

Kaeng Jud Thao Hu is the Thai version of breakfast granola.

4 to 6 servings

5 cups Thai Chicken Broth (page 34) or chicken stock
2 or 3 garlic cloves
½ cup fish sauce
½ teaspoon coarsely ground black pepper
½ pound ground pork
2 coriander stems with roots, finely chopped
2 bean curd cakes, cut into ½-inch cubes
2 scallions, chopped

In a medium-size pot, bring the chicken broth to a simmer. With a mortar and pestle, mash the garlic with ½ teaspoon of fish sauce and the black pepper. In a small bowl, combine the garlic–fish sauce mixture with the ground pork. Shape into small meatballs, about ½ inch in size. Bring the chicken broth to a boil and add the meatballs and coriander. Simmer for 5 minutes. Reduce the heat and add the bean curd cubes. Add the remaining fish sauce and serve, garnished with chopped scallions.

BEEF SOUP
Soup Nuea

My husband, George, loves this easy-to-prepare soup. He likes to eat it American style, with bread and butter, as a complete meal.

4 to 6 servings

1 pound beef chuck, cut into 1-inch-square chunks (stewing beef)
3 large tomatoes, peeled, seeded and quartered
1 large yellow onion, thickly sliced
2 celery stalks, cut into ½-inch pieces
⅔ cup fish sauce

Put all of the ingredients in a large pot with 7 cups of water and heat to a boil. Continue boiling for 5 minutes, then reduce the heat and cover the pot. Simmer for about ½ hour, or until the beef is tender.

SPINACH SOUP WITH EGG
Kaeng Jud Phak Khom

4 to 6 servings

2 tablespoons minced garlic
1 tablespoon vegetable oil
5 cups Thai Chicken Broth (page 34) or chicken stock
⅔ cup fish sauce
1 tablespoon sugar
5 eggs, slightly beaten
5 cups fresh spinach leaves
1½ teaspoons coarsely ground black pepper
2 scallions, cut into ½-inch slices

Saute the garlic in the vegetable oil until it is light brown. Set aside. In a large pot, bring the chicken broth and 2 cups of water to a boil. Add the fish sauce and sugar. With a large spoon, swirl the boiling broth and slowly drizzle in the eggs. Continue swirling for 2 minutes, or until the eggs are cooked. Add the spinach leaves and pepper, cover and reduce the heat. Continue simmering for 5 minutes. When ready to serve, stir in the scallions and float the sauteed garlic on top.

PINEAPPLE SOUP WITH PORK AND DRIED SHRIMP
Kaeng-Jud-Sab-Pha-Lot

4 to 6 servings

½ cup dried shrimp
2 tablespoons minced garlic
1 tablespoon vegetable oil
1 pound pork loin, cut into 1-inch cubes
⅔ cup fish sauce
1 cup fresh pineapple, cut into ½-inch cubes
2 teaspoons coarsely ground black pepper
2 scallions, chopped

Soak the dried shrimp in ½ cup of cold water for 10 minutes. Drain and set aside. Saute the garlic in the vegetable oil until it is light brown. Set aside. In a large pot, bring to a boil 9½ cups of water, than add the pork and fish sauce. Continue boiling for 7 to 10 minutes, or until the pork has cooked. Add the pineapple, pepper and shrimp. Cover, reduce the heat and simmer for 5 to 7 minutes. When ready to serve, stir in the scallions and float the sauteed garlic on top.

VEGETABLE SOUP WITH SPARERIBS
Tom Jrap-Chai

Thai food is rarely reheated because of the delicate nature of the spices used in cooking, but Tom Jrap-Chai is the exception. It is often made in large vats and reheated again and again over several days, with more vegetables and water added as needed. I start out with three kinds of cabbage: bok choy (Chinese cabbage), celery cabbage (Napa cabbage) and green leaf or white cabbage (the type most commonly found in supermarkets). If you cannot find bok choy or celery cabbage, just use the green leaf or white cabbage, tripling the amount. Add the bean thread noodles (woon sen), only to the portion you're serving, because they cook quickly and do not reheat well.

4 to 6 servings

4 to 6 garlic cloves, minced
2 tablespoons vegetable oil
1 medium white turnip, peeled and cut into ½-inch slices
2 cups bok choy (Chinese cabbage), cut into 1-inch slices
2 cups celery cabbage (Napa cabbage), cut into large chunks
2 cups green leaf cabbage, cut into large chunks
4 scallions, cut into 1-inch slices
½ cup black soy sauce
2 teaspoons coarsely ground black pepper
2 tablespoons sugar
1½ pounds spareribs, separated and cut into 1-inch pieces
2 tablespoons fish sauce
One 4-ounce package bean thread noodles

In a large pot, saute the garlic in the vegetable oil until it is light brown. Add the turnip, cabbages and scallions. Saute for 5 minutes. Add 10 cups of water, black soy sauce, pepper and sugar. When the soup begins to boil, add the spareribs. Bring to a boil again, add the fish sauce, cover and reduce the heat to a simmer. Cook for 30 minutes. Just before the soup is ready to serve, add the bean thread noodles and simmer for 2 to 3 minutes, or until they are soft.

TREE FUNGUS SOUP WITH GROUND PORK
Kaeng-Jud Hed-Nu

Tree fungus or black fungus is found in Oriental groceries, packaged like dried mushrooms, which are in the same family. Tree fungus is a common ingredient in many Oriental cuisines, added for texture and color rather than distinct flavor. In Thai cooking it is used in soups and mixed vegetable dishes.

4 to 6 servings

¼ cup dried tree fungus
2 pounds ground pork
3 tablespoons chopped garlic
⅔ cup fish sauce
2 teaspoons sugar
2 teaspoons coarsely ground black pepper
1 tablespoon vegetable oil
2 scallions, chopped

Soak the tree fungus in ½ cup of cold water for 10 minutes. Drain, and soak again in ½ cup of cold water for another 10 minutes. After draining the water the second time, rinse well, making certain no sand is left in the fungus. Set aside. In a large bowl, mix the ground pork with 1 tablespoon chopped garlic, 2 tablespoons fish sauce, 1 teaspoon sugar and ½ teaspoon black pepper. Allow the mixture to sit for ½ hour.

Saute the remaining garlic in the vegetable oil until it is light brown. Remove from the heat and set aside. Shape the pork mixture into 1-inch meatballs. Bring to a boil 6 cups of water, then add the pork meatballs. Add the remaining fish sauce, sugar and pepper. Return to a boil. Add the tree fungus, cover the pot and reduce the heat. Continue to simmer without stirring for 7 to 10 minutes. When ready to serve, gently fold in the scallions and float the sauteed garlic on top.

RICE
Khow

Rice is the center of any Thai meal. Rice is so important to Thai culture that the word for rice, khow, *is a synonym for food. In Thailand, instead of saying "let's eat," we say, "gin khow," which means "eat rice!"*

We use two types of rice, long-grain and short-grain, or glutinous, rice. Long-grain rice is the staple, eaten at every meal. Short-grain rice is used in desserts.

Rice is prepared by steaming, and there are three methods we use. The first calls for an electric rice steamer, which is a good investment if you plan on cooking rice frequently. Simply follow the manufacturer's instructions. The second method is to soak the rice in water overnight and cook it the next day over low heat until all of the grains are soft. The third method—the one given here because it is the fastest—is to cook the rice over high heat until most of the water has been absorbed, then complete the steaming process over low heat.

STEAMED RICE
Khow Sook

3 cups

1½ cups long-grain rice

Rinse the rice until the water runs clear. Put the rice and 2½ cups of water in a large pot. Cook over high heat, uncovered, until most of the water has been absorbed. (The surface of the rice should look moist.) Cover and reduce the heat as low as possible. Steam for approximately 20 minutes. The rice is done when a grain is soft enough to mash between your thumb and forefinger. Fluff the cooked rice with a fork and serve.

FRIED RICE
Khow Pad

Fried rice is usually served at lunch in Thailand, a practical way of using leftover rice from the night before. If you don't have leftover rice and have to start from scratch, be sure to allow enough time for the cooked rice to cool to room temperature, or it will not fry properly. The following recipes are typical of the way we eat Thai fried rice, but use your imagination when cooking these dishes, too. A Thai cook will add ingredients that are on hand, and so should you.

CRABMEAT FRIED RICE
Khow Pad Puu

4 to 6 servings

8 to 10 garlic cloves, finely chopped
¼ cup vegetable oil
½ pound crabmeat, torn into bite-size pieces
3 medium eggs, lightly beaten
1 medium onion, halved and thinly sliced
3 cups cooked rice
½ cup fish sauce
2 teaspoons sugar
1 teaspoon crushed red pepper
1 lemon, cut into wedges
1 cucumber, peeled and thinly sliced
1 large tomato, cut into wedges
Coriander leaves for garnish

In a wok or large skillet, stir-fry the garlic in the oil over low heat for about 5 minutes, or until the garlic is light brown. Quickly stir in the crabmeat. Continue stirring and add the beaten eggs and onion. When the egg has scrambled, turn the heat up to high and add the rice, fish sauce and sugar. Stir until all of the ingredients are well mixed and thoroughly cooked. Remove from the heat and stir in the crushed red pepper. Serve on a large platter, decorated with the lemon wedges, cucumber slices and tomato wedges. Garnish with coriander leaves.

PINEAPPLE FRIED RICE
Khow Pat Prik Sapbhalot

This is an example of chan nung—classic Thai cooking: as lovely to look at as it is to eat. I learned this recipe in Bangkok, and I often serve it at dinner parties to the oohs and ahs of my guests.

4 to 6 servings

1 large ripe pineapple (about 3½ to 4 pounds)
¼ cup vegetable oil
1 tablespoon Red Curry Paste (page 22)
1½ cups unsweetened coconut milk
½ pound pork loin, cut into bite-size chunks
½ pound shrimp, shelled and deveined
4 cups cooked rice
2 small green or red peppers, diced
1 tablespoon finely chopped fresh Oriental basil or mint leaves
2 or 3 dried lemon leaves, crushed, or 1 teaspoon grated lemon zest
2 teaspoons sugar
½ cup fish sauce
4 or 5 whole Oriental basil or mint leaves for garnish

Preheat the oven to 350° F. Cut the top off the pineapple, making a decorative pattern, such as a zigzag, at the crown. Being careful not to puncture the flesh, cut a thin slice off the bottom so the pineapple stands flat. Scoop out the pineapple pulp and chop about ¾ cup for the fried rice. Set the chopped pineapple and the pineapple shell aside until ready to use.

In a wok or frying pan, heat the oil and curry paste over medium heat for 3 minutes. Add 2 tablespoons of coconut milk. Add the pork chunks and cook for another 3 minutes, until it loses its pink color. Fold in the shrimp and stir, making sure all of the ingredients are thoroughly coated. Increase the heat to high and fold in the rice, pineapple pulp, peppers, chopped Oriental basil or mint, lemon leaves, sugar, fish sauce and remaining coconut milk. Continue stirring for 3 to 5 minutes, or until all of the ingredients are thoroughly mixed. Stuff the pineapple shell with the fried rice mixture, packing tightly. Bake for 20 minutes. Garnish with remaining whole basil or mint leaves and serve.

CURRIED RICE
Khow Phat Pong Kali

Curried rice is an excellent side dish that uses leftover rice. It is a perfect complement to dishes that do not have heavy sauces, such as the Marinated Chicken on page 72 or the Fish Cakes on page 106.

4 to 6 servings

1 medium onion, halved and thinly sliced
½ cup unsweetened coconut milk
1 tablespoon fish sauce
2 teaspoons yellow curry powder
3 cups cooked rice
½ cup fresh or frozen peas (if frozen, thaw first)

Simmer the onion in the coconut milk for 5 minutes, or until the onion becomes translucent and soft. Add the fish sauce and curry powder. Stir until everything is thoroughly mixed and the curry powder has dissolved. Fold in the rice and peas, cover and cook for another 5 minutes. Serve steaming hot.

SHRIMP PASTE FRIED RICE
Khow Krook Kapi

Khow Krook Kapi is always eaten as a side dish, usually served with pork. Try it with Sweet Pork (page 86). Shrimp paste has a distinct, pungent flavor that for the uninitiated palate might take some getting used to. Use it sparingly when preparing this dish.

Top the rice with several or all of the suggested condiments, or serve the condiments in small dishes on the side and let your guests choose the toppings they prefer.

4 to 6 servings

½ cup vegetable oil
½ cup dried shrimp
7 or 8 garlic cloves, finely chopped
2 tablespoons shrimp paste
1 tablespoon sugar
3 cups cooked rice
1 lemon, cut into wedges

CONDIMENTS AND TOPPINGS
3 eggs, scrambled and torn into bite-size pieces
¼ cup finely chopped shallots
2 fresh green chili peppers, seeded and finely chopped
1 cucumber, peeled and thinly sliced
1 green (unripe) mango or green apple, julienned

In a wok or frying pan, heat 2 tablespoons of oil and add the dried shrimp. Saute over low heat for 5 to 7 minutes. With a slotted spoon, remove the shrimp and set it aside to serve with the other condiments.

Add the remaining oil and chopped garlic. Stir-fry over low heat until the garlic is light brown. Add the shrimp paste and continue stirring for another 3 to 4 minutes. Add the sugar and stir until dissolved in the shrimp paste mixture. Fold in the rice, raise the heat and continue cooking and stirring until the rice is thoroughly coated and steaming. Garnish with the lemon wedges. Top with the condiments or serve them on the side.

CURRIED BEEF FRIED RICE
Khow Pad Nam Prik Kang Nuea

4 to 6 servings

2 tablespoons Panang Curry Paste (page 24)
¼ cup vegetable oil
1½ pounds round steak or flank steak, cut into 1-inch-long strips
3 or 4 lemon leaves, crushed, or 1 teaspoon grated lemon zest
¼ cup fish sauce
3 cups steamed rice
½ cup fresh or frozen peas (if frozen, thaw first)

In a wok or large frying pan, cook the curry paste and oil over medium heat for 2 minutes, until blended. Add the beef and crushed lemon leaves and cook for 5 to 7 minutes. Stir in the fish sauce and coat the beef. Fold in the rice, making sure all of the ingredients are thoroughly mixed. Add the peas and cook for another 5 to 7 minutes.

PORK FRIED RICE WITH CHILI PEPPERS
Khow Moo Pad Prik

4 to 6 servings

5 to 7 garlic cloves, chopped
¼ cup vegetable oil
1½ pounds pork loin, sliced thin in 1-inch-long strips
3 cups cooked rice
½ cup fish sauce
1 tablespoon sugar
2 fresh green chili peppers, seeded and thinly sliced on the diagonal
½ cup chopped fresh Oriental basil leaves or mint leaves
Coriander leaves, Oriental basil or mint leaves for garnish

In a wok or large frying pan, stir-fry the garlic in the oil until it is light brown. Add the pork and stir-fry for about 7 to 8 minutes, or until no longer pink. Over high heat, fold in the rice, fish sauce and sugar. Stir-fry for another 5 minutes, or until all ingredients are cooked. Add the chili peppers and chopped basil, mixing well. Arrange the rice on a large platter, garnish with coriander, Oriental basil or mint leaves and serve.

SHRIMP FRIED RICE
Khow Pad Koong

4 to 6 servings

4 or 5 garlic cloves, chopped
¼ cup vegetable oil
1½ pounds small shrimp, shelled and deveined
3 eggs
½ cup fish sauce
2 teaspoons sugar
2 scallions, cut into ½-inch slices
½ teaspoon crushed red pepper
1 cucumber, peeled and thinly sliced
Coriander leaves for garnish

In a wok or large frying pan, stir-fry the garlic in oil until it is light brown. Over medium heat, add the shrimp and stir-fry for 2 to 3 minutes. In a small bowl, quickly beat the eggs with 1 tablespoon fish sauce and 1 teaspoon sugar. Stir this mixture into the shrimp. When the egg starts to cook, add the rice and remaining fish sauce and sugar. Stir well until all of the ingredients are thoroughly mixed. Reduce the heat and add the scallions and crushed pepper. Arrange on a large platter, topped with cucumber slices and garnished with coriander leaves.

APPETIZERS AND SALADS
Khong Wang Leh Salut

Appetizers are generally reserved for special occasions. They are not part of everyday Thai fare, although many of the dishes in this chapter are served as side dishes with the meal: Crabmeat Fritters (page 58) and Marinated Beef on Skewers (page 62), for example. The concept of separate courses, however, is not part of Thai culture, unless the meal is so large, as in religious and wedding banquets, that the only practical way of serving is to present many courses—and that's an all-day affair!

Khong wang are most often prepared as hors d'oeuvres for the men's gatherings. These evening meetings are a regular part of Thai life, especially in the villages. The men get together to discuss politics, play cards and socialize.

Like khong wang, salads are rarely served as a separate course, and the presence of a special yum salut *usually highlights a celebratory occasion.*

CURRIED CHICKEN TURNOVERS
Kha Li Pap Gai

I learned to make these delicious turnovers when I was living with my older sister in Bangkok, which is why I always think of them as a city or sophisticated dish. Kha Li Pap Gai are very easy to prepare and can be frozen uncooked for a month. They are delicious served with Cucumber Salad (page 65).

Approximately 1 dozen

FILLING
½ pound boneless chicken breast, diced
1 cup potatoes, peeled and diced
½ cup chopped onions
1 teaspoon Masaman Curry Paste (page 23)
2 tablespoons sugar
2 tablespoons fish sauce

In a medium-size pot, bring 1½ cups of water to a boil. Add the chicken and simmer for 8 to 10 minutes, or until the chicken is cooked. Remove the chicken with a slotted spoon. Add the diced potatoes to the stock and simmer for 7 to 8 minutes, or until tender. Return the chicken to the pot, add the remaining ingredients and simmer, uncovered, until the liquid is absorbed. Remove from the heat and let cool. The filling can be made a day in advance and refrigerated.

PASTRY
2 cups all-purpose flour
1 teaspoon salt
⅔ cup vegetable shortening, chilled

Sift the flour and salt together in a large mixing bowl. Using a pastry cutter or two forks, cut in the chilled shortening until the dough has the texture of coarse meal. Sprinkle in 5 to 6 tablespoons of cold water, adding a tablespoon at a time until a ball of dough is formed. Divide the dough ball into two pieces for easier handling. With a rolling pin, roll each ball of pastry into a rectangle approximately 12 by 8 inches. Cut the dough into six squares, each approximately 4 inches square.

ASSEMBLING
1 large egg

Preheat the oven to 400° F. Lightly beat the egg with 1 tablespoon of cold water. Place 1 heaping tablespoon of the filling on half of a pastry square. Brush the edges with the egg mixture, fold to make a triangle and pinch closed. Brush the top of each turnover with the egg mixture. (Eliminate this step if freezing the turnovers before they are baked.) Bake the turnovers on a baking sheet or in a flat baking dish for 15 minutes, or until they are golden brown.

FRITTERS
Tod Krob

In my travels, I've found that almost every country has its own version of a fried dough or fritter dish; the Italians have calzone, the French eat beignets, Americans eat apple fritters and hush puppies, and so on. In Thailand, spicy fritters laden with seafood or vegetables are eaten as snacks, appetizers or side dishes at dinner.

CRABMEAT FRITTERS
Nueapu Tod Krob

Approximately 1 dozen

½ cup all-purpose flour
1 teaspoon baking powder
1 teaspoon baking soda
1 teaspoon sugar
3 eggs, lightly beaten
1 tablespoon Red Curry Paste (page 22)
1 lemon leaf, crushed, or ½ teaspoon grated lemon zest
1½ tablespoons fish sauce
1 pound crabmeat, fresh or frozen
1½ cups vegetable oil for frying

Sift the flour, baking powder, baking soda and sugar together into a bowl. Stir in the eggs, red curry paste, lemon leaf and fish sauce. Mix thoroughly until a thick, sticky batter is formed. Tear the crabmeat into bite-size pieces and fold into the batter.

In a wok or large deep frying pan, heat the oil until it begins to smoke. Drop the batter by heaping tablespoonsful into the hot oil. Brown for 3 minutes per side, or until golden. Do not crowd the pan or the fritters will not brown evenly. Drain the fritters on paper towels before serving.

CORN FRITTERS
Khao Pud Tod

Approximately 1 dozen

2 cups whole corn kernels (approximately 4 large ears or one
    16-ounce can vacuum-packed corn)
½ cup all-purpose flour
1 teaspoon baking powder
1 teaspoon baking soda
1 teaspoon sugar
2 medium eggs, lightly beaten
1 tablespoon Red Curry Paste (page 22)
1 lemon leaf, crushed, or ½ teaspoon grated lemon zest
¼ teaspoon coarsely ground black pepper
4 garlic cloves, finely chopped
1 tablespoon fish sauce
1½ cups vegetable oil

Put the corn in a bowl and with the back of a spoon lightly press the
kernels to crush them slightly and render their liquid. Set aside. In a
large mixing bowl, sift the flour, baking powder, baking soda and
sugar together. Add the eggs, red curry paste, lemon leaf, black
pepper, garlic cloves and fish sauce. Mix well. Fold the corn and
liquid into the batter. Mix thoroughly until a thick, lumpy batter with
a slightly sticky consistency like pancake batter is formed.

    In a wok or large deep frying pan, heat the oil until it is almost
smoking. Drop the batter in by heaping tablespoonsful and fry on
each side for approximately 3 minutes, or until golden. Drain the
fritters on paper towels and serve.

TAPIOCA BALLS
Saku Sai Mu

Tapioca balls are a traditional Thai appetizer. They can be prepared ahead and kept in the refrigerator for 24 hours, or the filling can be prepared in advance and frozen for 2 months. Hua chai po, or pickled turnips, give Saku Sai Mu their unique flavor and can be purchased in any Oriental grocery, but if you cannot find them, make the tapioca balls anyway—they will still be delicious!

Approximately 2 dozen

FILLING
10 garlic cloves, finely chopped
¼ cup vegetable oil
¾ pound ground pork
¼ cup coarsely chopped pickled turnips (optional)
¼ cup crushed unsalted peanuts
1 teaspoon coarsely ground black pepper
2 tablespoons fish sauce
¼ cup palm sugar or light brown sugar

In a frying pan over medium heat, cook the garlic in the oil until it is light brown. Reserve 1 teaspoon of the browned garlic to use as a garnish. Add the ground pork to the remaining garlic and stir-fry until the pork is no longer pink and is thoroughly cooked. Stir in the pickled turnips, peanuts, black pepper, fish sauce and sugar. Reduce the heat and continue cooking until the mixture is well combined and sticky. Set aside and allow to cool while preparing the dough.

DOUGH
3 cups small pearl tapioca

Place the tapioca and enough water to cover it, approximately 3 to 4 cups, in a mixing bowl. Soak for 2 to 3 minutes and drain. Place the moistened tapioca in a saucepan over low heat. Add 1 to 2 cups of water and cook for 5 minutes, or until the water has been completely absorbed. Remove from the heat and let the tapioca dough stand until it is cool enough to handle.

ASSEMBLING

The tapioca dough will be very sticky and difficult to handle at first. I keep a bowl of ice-cold water next to my work area and constantly moisten my hands to make working with the dough easier. Or another method is to roll the dough between two layers of plastic wrap.

Drop a heaping tablespoon of the dough onto a smooth, nonporous surface. (The dough should be slightly tepid to the touch, not too hot or too cold.) With the heel of the hand, spread the dough into a paper-thin circle, measuring approximately 3 to 3½ inches in diameter. Place a level teaspoon of the ground pork mixture in the center of the circle. Pinch the edges of the dough together to form a ball, with all of the edges meeting at the top. Pinch the top closed.

STEAMING

Coat a steamer, bamboo or metal, with a thin layer of vegetable oil to prevent sticking. Arrange the tapioca balls, pinched side down, on the steamer, far enough apart so they don't touch each other. Cover and steam for 10 to 12 minutes, or until the balls look translucent. Remove the balls from the steamer, sprinkle the remaining browned garlic over the tops and serve warm.

MARINATED BEEF ON SKEWERS
Sate Nuea

Sate (pronounced "sah-tay") is one of Thailand's best-known dishes. Strips of meat are marinated in a curry–coconut milk mixture and then grilled or broiled on skewers. I prefer to marinate them over- night, but 5 hours is enough time to impart the wonderful flavors of the marinade.

Use the 12-inch-long bamboo sticks to skewer the meat; they are the most attractive for serving sate. Bamboo sticks are available at Orien- tal groceries and cookware shops. Soak the bamboo sticks in water for at least 2 hours to keep them from burning.

Sate is traditionally served with a peanut–coconut milk sauce for dipping, called Nam Jim Sate, and Cucumber Salad (page 65). You can substitute strips of boneless pork loin or boneless chicken breasts for the beef. To serve it as a main course just double the recipe.

4 servings

1½ cups unsweetened coconut milk
1 tablespoon Red Curry Paste (page 22)
1 tablespoon fish sauce
2 teaspoons curry powder
1 pound round steak or flank steak, sliced into long narrow strips, 1
    inch wide x 3 inches long (this will give you 24 to 32 strips)

In a long flat dish, mix the coconut milk, red curry paste, fish sauce and curry powder together. Add the beef strips and marinate them in the refrigerator for at least 5 hours, or overnight.

Preheat the broiler or outdoor grill. Weave 2 strips of meat onto each skewer, lengthwise. There will be approximately 12 to 16 skew- ers. Broil or grill for 5 minutes on each side. Serve with the Nam Jim Sate.

PEANUT–COCONUT MILK DIPPING SAUCE
Nam Jim Sate
1½ cups unsweetened coconut milk
1 tablespoon Red Curry Paste (page 22)
½ cup unsalted chunky-style peanut butter
1½ tablespoons white vinegar
2 tablespoons sugar
1 tablespoon fish sauce

Heat ¾ cup coconut milk in a saucepan. Add the red curry paste and stir until the mixture is pale amber and a coating of oil appears on the surface. Add the peanut butter, vinegar, sugar, fish sauce and remaining coconut milk. Continue cooking, stirring for 8 to 10 minutes, or until the sauce has thickened slightly. Allow the sauce to cool slightly and serve with the sate.

Note: The dipping sauce may be prepared a week in advance and reheated when you are ready to serve the sate.

THAI SALAD
Salad Kak

Thai salad is wonderful as a side dish or as a balanced meal by itself thanks to the combination of bean curd, vegetables and peanuts. In Thailand it is served topped with crunchy homemade potato chips, but commercial chips will do.

4 to 6 servings

1 large head iceberg or romaine lettuce, torn into bite-size chunks
2 medium tomatoes, quartered
1 small red onion, thinly sliced
1 medium carrot, thinly sliced
1 cucumber, peeled and thinly sliced
1 firm-style bean curd square, cut into ¼-inch cubes
1 hard-cooked egg, finely chopped
1 cup mung bean sprouts
1 small bag potato chips or potato sticks (optional)

Arrange the lettuce, tomatoes, onion, carrot and cucumber in a salad bowl and lightly toss. Add the bean curd, chopped egg and mung bean sprouts. Top with the peanut–coconut milk dressing and garnish with potato chips or potato sticks.

PEANUT–COCONUT MILK SALAD DRESSING
Nam Salad Kak
1½ cups unsweetened coconut milk
1 tablespoon Red Curry Paste (page 22)
2 cups unsalted chunky-style peanut butter
½ cup white vinegar
2 tablespoons sugar
1½ tablespoons fish sauce

In a saucepan over medium heat, stir the coconut milk and red curry paste together until the mixture turns pale amber and a thin coat of oil appears on the surface. Add the remaining ingredients and stir over low heat for 7 to 10 minutes, or until all of the ingredients are thoroughly mixed. The color will be a pale cocoa brown. Let cool at room temperature for 1 hour before serving with the salad.

Note: This dressing will keep in the refrigerator for a month, but it does have a tendency to thicken. To bring it back to the right consistency, add ½ teaspoon to 1 tablespoon white vinegar and vigorously stir.

CUCUMBER SALAD
Thangua Dong

Thangua Dong is a spicy yet sweet cucumber salad, usually served as a side dish with Marinated Chicken and Marinated Beef on Skewers.

4 to 6 servings

1 cup white vinegar
¼ cup sugar
1 large cucumber, halved lengthwise, peeled, seeded and thinly
    sliced
1 small red onion, halved and thinly sliced
1 large carrot, peeled and thinly sliced
½ sweet bell pepper, red or green, julienned
¼ teaspoon crushed red pepper

In a small saucepan heat the vinegar and sugar for 5 minutes, or until the sugar has completely dissolved. Let the mixture cool completely. Put the remaining ingredients in a bowl and add the vinegar mixture. The salad is best if marinated for at least 2 hours. It will keep in the refrigerator for 1 week.

MIXED SALAD
Yam Yai

Yam Yai is a mixed salad of meats and mung bean thread noodles. In Thailand it is often made with leftover seafood and meats. One ingredient, called tree fungus, is used primarily for texture. It can be found in Oriental groceries and some supermarkets, and is also sold as cloud ears and tree ears. If tree fungus is unavailable, substitute dried mushrooms.

4 to 6 servings

5 fresh red chili peppers, seeded
½ cup fish sauce
10 garlic cloves, peeled
½ cup lemon juice
2 teaspoons sugar
½ teaspoon salt
3 coriander roots
¼ cup dried tree fungus
1 bunch (4 ounces) mung bean thread noodles
1 large cucumber, peeled, halved lengthwise, seeded and sliced
1 head celery cabbage (Napa cabbage) or iceberg lettuce, shredded
3 coriander stems, finely chopped
¼ pound boneless pork loin, cooked and sliced into thin strips
½ pound boneless chicken, cooked and cut into bite-size chunks
¼ pound calf's liver, cooked and sliced into thin strips
1 pound shrimp, shelled, deveined and cooked
1 small bunch Oriental basil or mint leaves (approximately 10 leaves)
1 large hard-cooked egg, cut into wedges
Coriander leaves for garnish

Put the chili peppers, fish sauce and garlic into a mortar, with a pestle or in a food processor and mash into a paste. Add the lemon juice, sugar, salt and coriander roots. Continue mixing and mashing until a dark red paste is formed. Transfer the mixture to a large bowl and set aside until ready to use. In two separate bowls, soak the tree fungus and mung bean thread noodles in cold water for 15 minutes.

Meanwhile, add the cucumber, Chinese cabbage or lettuce and chopped coriander stems to the large bowl of sauce. Stir well, coating the vegetables. Drain the tree fungus and bean threads well and add them to the bowl of sauce and vegetables. Stir and coat well. Add the pork, chicken, liver and shrimp. Again stir well, completely coating all of the ingredients. Stir in the Oriental basil or mint leaves. Let the salad marinate for ½ hour before serving. Place all of the ingredients on a large platter, and decoratively arrange the egg wedges and coriander leaves around the salad before serving.

LETTUCE LEAVES STUFFED WITH SHRIMP AND COCONUT
Miang Kam

Miang Kam is a traditional Thai hors d'oeuvre usually served at parties or festivals. A mixture of dried shrimp and a special sauce, it is placed on lettuce leaves. To eat it, simply fold the lettuce leaf over the filling and pop it into your mouth.

Approximately 2 dozen

1½ cups diced or shredded coconut, fresh or dried
¾ cup dried shrimp
½ cup chopped fresh ginger
1 lime, peeled, seeded and chopped
3 fresh red chili peppers, seeded and thinly sliced on the diagonal
2 heads soft leaf lettuce, such as romaine, red leaf or butter
1 tablespoon shrimp paste
¼ cup ground unsalted peanuts
¼ cup palm sugar or light brown sugar
¼ cup fish sauce

In a dry skillet over low heat, toast ½ cup of coconut until it is light brown. (If you are using dried coconut, soak it in cold water for 5 minutes, drain thoroughly and then toast it.) In a bowl, combine the toasted coconut, shrimp, ginger, lime and chili peppers. Set aside. Separate, clean and pat dry the lettuce leaves. Arrange the lettuce leaves on large platters, allowing enough space for easy handling.

In a saucepan over medium heat, combine the shrimp paste, peanuts, sugar, fish sauce and remaining coconut. Cook for 7 to 10 minutes, or until the sauce is syrupy. Set aside to cool for ½ hour. When ready to serve, place a heaping teaspoon of the dried shrimp filling in the center of each lettuce leaf. Top with ½ teaspoon of the slightly warm sauce.

FRIED RICE STICKS WITH TAMARIND SAUCE
Mee Krob

Mee Krob is made with sen mee noodles, also known as rice sticks or rice vermicelli. Sen mee are available in Oriental groceries and many supermarkets carrying Oriental products. If you have an Oriental section in your local supermarket, look for mai fun—the Chinese name.

In this dish the sen mee noodles are deep fried without first being soaked in water. Sen mee noodles come packaged in small bunches, one to three per package. If your package contains three bunches, separate them first and fry one at a time.

The sauce may be prepared up to a week in advance. When combining it with the sen mee, make sure it is slightly warm but not hot, or the noodles will become soft and mushy.

4 servings

¼ pound dried or frozen tamarind pods
3¼ cups vegetable oil
½ cup minced shallots
5 or 6 garlic cloves, chopped
¼ cup black bean sauce
¼ pound ground pork or veal
⅓ cup tomato paste
½ cup sugar
1 pound shrimp, shelled and deveined
3 bundles sen mee rice sticks (approximately 8 ounces)
½ cup mung bean sprouts
Coriander leaves for garnish

Soak the tamarind pods in ½ cup cold water for 1 hour. Discard the pods and reserve the liquid. (If using tamarind syrup, omit this step and decrease the sugar to ¼ cup.)

In a large wok or frying pan, heat ¼ cup of the oil, add the shallots and stir-fry them for 3 to 5 minutes, or until lightly browned. Add the garlic and stir-fry for another 2 to 3 minutes. Add the black bean sauce and ground pork or veal and continue cooking for 5 minutes, stirring to coat the meat. Stir in the tomato paste, sugar and reserved tamarind liquid. Continue stirring until the sauce has thickened, about 7 minutes. Add the shrimp and cook for another 3 minutes. Remove the sauce from the heat. Set aside to cool.

In another wok or frying pan, heat the remaining 3 cups of oil until smoking. Drop in the rice sticks, one bundle at a time, and fry for 2 to 3 minutes, or until the noodles swell and become opaque. Add the noodles to the sauce, thoroughly coating them. Arrange on a platter and garnish with the bean sprouts and coriander leaves.

CHICKEN AND DUCK
Gai Leh Pbet

My family had a chicken coop behind the house—far behind the house. My youngest brother was in charge of cleaning it, and he was always trying to con me into helping him. So I helped him feed the chickens instead. In Thailand we feed our chickens coconut pulp left over from making coconut milk. It's economical and gives the meat a wonderful flavor. We also dry the pulp and spread it on the floor of the coop to take away some of the strong odor.

HOME-STYLE MARINATED CHICKEN
Gai Yang

Gai Yang is a very popular dish in Thailand; it is everyday fare—so easy and so delicious. It is simply marinated chicken that is either grilled, or baked and then broiled for a few moments. The chicken can be marinated one or two days in advance, so it's an ideal dish to cook after a busy day.

Every Thai cook has at least two recipes for Gai Yang, and I've included my two favorites. Serve this dish with Dipping Sauce (recipe follows), Cucumber Salad (page 65) and, as always, rice.

4 servings

1 cup unsweetened coconut milk
½ cup fish sauce
1 tablespoon Red Curry Paste (page 22)
1 tablespoon yellow curry powder
1 tablespoon cracked black peppercorns
2 tablespoons sugar
3 or 4 coriander stems with roots, finely chopped
Two 2½- to 3-pound broilers, halved lengthwise

Thoroughly mix the coconut milk, fish sauce, red curry paste and yellow curry powder in a bowl. Add the black peppercorns, sugar and coriander. Place the chicken skin side down in a shallow baking dish. Pour the marinade over the chicken. Cover the dish, refrigerate and marinate for at least 7 hours.

Preheat the oven to 350° F. and bake the chicken, uncovered, in the marinade for 40 to 50 minutes, depending upon the size. Just before serving, place the chicken under the broiler for 5 minutes, or until the skin becomes crisp. Cut the chicken halves into 4 pieces and serve with individual side dishes of dipping sauce.

DIPPING SAUCE
Nam Jim Gai Yang
2 fresh red chili peppers, seeded and chopped
½ cup chopped preserved or pickled garlic
1 small onion, quartered

¼ cup white wine vinegar
1 tablespoon salt
1½ cups sugar

In a large saucepan, simmer all of the ingredients with 3½ cups of cold water for 40 minutes. Strain, reserving the liquid, and mash the rest of the ingredients to a thick pastelike consistency. In a saucepan, heat the mashed ingredients over low heat. Slowly add the liquid and stir until the sauce thickens slightly.

MARINATED CHICKEN
Gai Yang

4 servings

1 tablespoon Red Curry Paste (page 22)
1 cup light soy sauce
3 or 4 coriander stems with roots, finely chopped
7 or 8 garlic cloves, finely chopped
2 tablespoons finely chopped fresh ginger
1 carrot, chopped
2 celery stalks, chopped
1 small onion, chopped
¼ cup vegetable oil
¼ cup cracked black peppercorns
Two 2½- to 3-pound broilers, halved lengthwise

Mix all of the ingredients except the chicken in a bowl. Make sure the curry paste is thoroughly blended with the soy sauce. Place the chicken skin side down in a shallow baking dish. Pour the marinade over the chicken. Cover, refrigerate and marinate for at least 7 hours.

Preheat the oven to 350°F. Bake the chicken, uncovered, in the marinade for 40 to 50 minutes, depending upon the size. Just before serving, place the chicken under the broiler for 5 minutes, or until the skin is crisp. Cut the chicken halves into 4 pieces and serve with the dipping sauce on the side.

CHICKEN AND CHICKEN LIVERS IN RED CURRY SAUCE
Gang Gai

Gang Gai is a typical example of a kaeng, or gravy dish. It is usually served with Nam Prik Ma Muang (Green Mango and Shrimp Paste Sauce) and rice.

4 to 6 servings

2 cups unsweetened coconut milk
1 to 1½ tablespoons Red Curry Paste (depending on your taste) (page 22)
2 pounds boneless chicken breasts, cut into bite-size pieces
¼ cup fish sauce
3 or 4 lemon leaves, crushed, or 1½ teaspoon grated lemon zest
2 teaspoons sugar
1 pound chicken livers
2 fresh green chili peppers, seeded and thinly sliced on the diagonal
½ cup fresh or frozen peas, thawed, if frozen

In a large pot, heat ¼ coconut milk with the curry paste. Stir over low heat until the mixture is a dark amber liquid and a thin layer of oil coats the surface. Add the chicken and cook for 5 minutes. Stir in the remaining coconut milk, the fish sauce, lemon leaves and sugar. Cover, raise the heat to medium and cook for 10 minutes.

Remove the cover, add the chicken livers and simmer for 5 minutes. Before serving, stir in the chili peppers and peas. Cook for another 5 to 7 minutes.

SESAME CHICKEN WITH VEGETABLES
Gai Pad Pak

4 to 6 servings

½ cup dried mushrooms
½ cup all-purpose flour
2 teaspoons salt
2 teaspoons ground pepper
2 pounds boneless chicken breasts, cut into 1-inch strips
½ cup sesame oil
1 cup celery cabbage (Napa cabbage) cut into bite-size chunks
1 cup bok choy (Chinese cabbage) stems and leaves cut into 1½-inch
   pieces
1 medium red bell pepper, julienned
1 cup fresh snow peas
¾ cup canned baby corn (about 10 to 15 ears), halved lengthwise
2 tablespoons fish sauce
¾ cup Thai Chicken Broth (page 34) or chicken stock
1 tablespoon sugar
1½ tablespoons arrowroot powder
Coriander leaves for garnish

Soak the dried mushrooms in 2 cups of cold water for 20 minutes, or until softened. Drain and set aside. In a large mixing bowl, combine the flour, salt and pepper. Add the sliced chicken and coat well.

In a wok or large frying pan, heat the sesame oil until it begins to smoke. Add the coated chicken pieces and stir-fry to brown evenly, about 3 to 5 minutes. Add the mushrooms, celery cabbage, bok choy and red bell pepper. Stir over high heat vigorously, coating all of the vegetables. Add the snow peas and baby corn and continue stir-frying for another 2 to 3 minutes. Stir in the fish sauce, chicken stock and sugar. While the broth begins to simmer, dissolve the arrowroot in ¼ cup of hot water. Stir it into the simmering chicken and vegetables.

Lower the heat to medium and continue simmering, stirring occasionally, for 5 to 7 minutes, or until the sauce thickens. Serve in a large shallow serving bowl and garnish with coriander leaves.

CHICKEN CAKES
Tod Man Gai

Chicken cakes, similar to fish or crab cakes, are great for lunch or snacks or as an additional dish at dinner. They are usually served with Cucumber Salad (page 65) and rice. I have used this recipe since I lived in Bangkok with my older sister. The reason I mention this is because many people question my use of white bread. The fact of the matter is that we do have packaged bread in Thailand, although it is usually eaten with ice cream, for dessert. Here the bread is used to bind the chicken mixture together. The prepared chicken cakes can be refrigerated for up to 24 hours before they are cooked.

Approximately 1 dozen

2 or 3 fresh chili peppers, seeded and chopped
¼ cup fresh ginger, chopped
10 garlic cloves, peeled and chopped
1 teaspoon salt
8 slices white bread, crusts removed
2 pounds ground chicken
3 scallions, chopped
2 coriander stems with roots, finely chopped
2 cups vegetable oil
4 or 5 shallots, peeled and finely chopped
3 medium eggs, beaten
½ cup bread crumbs
Coriander leaves for garnish

Put the chili peppers, ginger, garlic and salt in a mortar with a pestle or in a food processor and mash completely. Set aside. Soak the bread in 1 cup of cold water for 2 to 3 minutes, until uniformly soft and wet. Squeeze the excess water out and place the wet bread in a large mixing bowl. Add the chili pepper paste and the ground chicken to the soaked bread, mixing it together well with your hands. Add the scallions and coriander and mix well.

 In a small skillet, heat 2 tablespoons of the vegetable oil, add the chopped shallots and saute until light brown. Add to the chicken mixture. Refrigerate for ½ hour for easier handling.

In a large frying pan, heat the remaining oil over medium to high heat until it begins to smoke. Shape approximately 2 tablespoons of the mixture into a pancake about 3 inches in diameter and ½ to ¾ inch thick. Dip the pancake into the beaten eggs, coat with the bread crumbs and fry until golden brown, about 6 to 8 minutes per side. Repeat this procedure, frying 4 or 5 cakes at a time until all the batter is used up. Arrange the cakes on a large platter, garnish with coriander leaves and serve with cucumber salad and rice.

CHICKEN IN GREEN CURRY
Gang Kaeo Wan Gai

4 to 6 servings

1½ cups unsweetened coconut milk
1½ tablespoons Green Curry Paste (page 25)
2½ pounds boneless chicken, sliced into 1-inch strips
1 cup sliced bamboo shoots
¼ cup fish sauce
1 tablespoon sugar
1 small bunch Oriental basil leaves or mint leaves, chopped
    (about ¼ cup)
2 fresh green chili peppers, seeded and thinly sliced on the diagonal

In a large saucepan, heat ¼ cup of coconut milk with the green curry paste. Stir until it is well blended and a thin coat of oil appears on the surface. Add the chicken and continue cooking over medium heat for 5 minutes, stirring constantly. Stir in the remaining coconut milk and the bamboo shoots, fish sauce and sugar. Cover and simmer for 8 to 10 minutes, or until the chicken is cooked. Remove the cover and stir in the Oriental basil leaves and chili peppers. Cook, stirring for 3 to 5 minutes. Serve with rice.

CAPON WITH BLACK BEAN SAUCE
Gai-Thong Tow Tchiow

My family is part Chinese and when we celebrate Chinese New Year we offer three bowls of food: one to our ancestors, one to the unknown spirits and one to the gods. Capon with black bean sauce is one of the dishes we offer to our ancestors. The ceremony includes lighting incense and saying prayers. When the incense has finally burned out, we joyously eat!

4 to 6 servings

12 garlic cloves, 6 cut in half and 6 finely chopped
One 6-pound whole capon, cleaned
2 cups uncooked long-grain rice
½ cup black bean sauce
¼ cup black soy sauce
2 tablespoons lemon juice
2 tablespoons finely minced fresh ginger
3 fresh red chili peppers, seeded and finely chopped
2 teaspoons sugar
2 tablespoons vegetable oil
1 large cucumber, peeled and thinly sliced
Coriander leaves for garnish

Fill a pot, large enough to cook the capon in, halfway with water, about 6 to 8 cups. Add the halved garlic cloves and bring to a boil. Put the capon in the pot, adding more water if needed to cover the bird. Cover and simmer over medium heat for 1 to 1½ hours, or until the capon is completely cooked and no blood appears when it is lightly pricked with a fork. Remove the cooked capon and set aside. Reserve 3 cups of stock in the large pot, add the rice and cover. Cook the rice for 20 minutes, lifting the cover to stir every 5 minutes so it doesn't burn. Reduce the heat to low and cook for another 5 minutes. Remove from heat, keep covered and let the rice continue steaming.

In a small saucepan, combine the black bean sauce, black soy sauce, lemon juice, fresh ginger, chili peppers and sugar. Simmer for

5 to 7 minutes. Cover and set aside, near the heat. In a small skillet, heat the oil and add the chopped garlic. Saute until the garlic turns light brown. Uncover the black bean sauce mixture and float the garlic and oil on top. Do not stir.

Remove the skin from the capon and slice the capon. Arrange the rice on a large platter. Place the sliced capon on top of the rice. Spoon the sauce on top of the capon, completely covering the meat. Place the cucumber slices around the platter decoratively and garnish with coriander leaves.

SAUTEED CHICKEN WITH ORIENTAL BASIL
Gai Pad Bai Kra Prow

If fresh Oriental basil is not available, substitute fresh mint leaves.

4 to 6 servings

½ cup vegetable oil
5 or 6 garlic cloves, finely chopped
2½ pounds boneless chicken, cut into 1-inch chunks
½ cup (2 small bunches) chopped Oriental basil leaves
½ teaspoon coarsely ground black pepper
2 fresh green chili peppers, seeded and thinly sliced on the diagonal
1½ tablespoons sugar
¼ cup fish sauce
1½ tablespoons black soy sauce

In a wok or large frying pan, heat the oil and stir-fry the garlic until it is light brown. Add the chicken and stir-fry over high heat for 6 to 8 minutes. Add the rest of the ingredients, reduce the heat to low and simmer for 10 to 15 minutes, or until the chicken is completely cooked. Serve with rice.

DUCK WITH PRESERVED LEMON
Phed Tun Ma-Nao Dong

My mother raised ducks and chickens, and there were always at least a dozen running around the yard. For some reason, though, my mother's ducks were very stubborn; they would consistently lay their eggs on our neighbors' property. For years we fought with these neighbors, who would not let us retrieve our ducks' eggs. They insisted: their property, their eggs. So we never ate duck eggs—only duck.

The main flavoring ingredient for this dish, preserved lemon, is sold in jars in Oriental groceries, like preserved garlic. It has a very strong flavor and is cooked wrapped in cheesecloth. If you cannot find preserved lemon, substitute ¼ cup of lemon juice, 2 tablespoons of lemon zest and double the amount of sugar used. You will obviously not need to use the cheesecloth. Preserved lemon has a very distinct tart-sweet flavor, so do try to use it.

4 to 6 servings

1 cup vegetable oil
Two 4-pound ducks, quartered
6 garlic cloves
1 teaspoon black peppercorns
4 coriander stems with roots
2 tablespoons fish sauce
2 tablespoons black soy sauce
1 tablespoon sugar
2 preserved lemon slices, wrapped in cheesecloth
2 tablespoons preserved lemon juice from the jar
2 large white turnips, peeled and cut into 1-inch cubes
Coriander leaves for garnish

In a large frying pan, heat the oil until it begins to smoke. Add the quartered ducks and fry, skin side down. Fry for 10 minutes, or until the skin turns brown and the fat under the skin begins to melt. Turn the duck over and fry for another 5 minutes. Remove the duck pieces and set aside.

Put 2 tablespoons of the hot oil with the garlic, peppercorns and coriander into a mortar with a pestle or in a food processor and mash into a paste. In a large pot, heat the paste over low heat for 2 to 3 minutes or until it begins to sizzle. Add the duck pieces, fish sauce, black soy sauce, sugar and 4 cups of cold water. When the liquid begins to simmer, put the preserved lemon in cheesecloth, preserved lemon juice and turnips in the pot. There should be enough liquid to cover all of the ingredients. If not, add water. Cover and cook over medium heat for 45 minutes, or until the duck is cooked and tender.

With a slotted spoon, remove the duck and turnips from the pot and arrange on a large platter. Spoon the sauce on top of the duck, serving the extra sauce on the side. Garnish with coriander leaves and serve with rice.

BAKED CHICKEN LEGS IN RED SAUCE
Kha-Gai Oeb Nam-Dang

This is one of my favorite dishes from my student days in Bangkok.

4 to 6 servings

12 to 15 chicken legs (drumsticks)
¼ cup Scotch whisky
2 tablespoons margarine, softened
¼ cup light soy sauce
1 tablespoon ground black pepper
2 coriander stems with roots, finely chopped
6 garlic cloves, finely chopped
½ cup all-purpose flour
½ cup vegetable oil
1 cup tomato sauce

Place the chicken legs in a large mixing bowl. Add the Scotch, margarine, soy sauce, pepper, coriander and garlic. Toss the ingredients so each leg is thoroughly coated. Cover and refrigerate for at least 7 hours, or overnight.

Preheat the oven to 400° F. Dredge the marinated chicken legs in the flour. In a large frying pan, heat the oil until it smokes. Add the chicken legs and brown them for 3 to 5 minutes on each side. Place the browned chicken legs in a deep baking dish. Add the tomato sauce and 1 cup of cold water. Bake for 25 minutes, or until the chicken legs are tender when pierced with a fork.

PORK
Moo

My parents' house is on a canal just off the famous floating market of Damnoen Sa-duak. When I was a child, the different vendors would pass by the house on the way to sell their wares at the market. At 6:00 A.M. we would hear the horn of the rruea-hang-youw, or boat with a long tail—the pork boat. The vendor of this small craft always made a special stop for my mother, and what a wonderful sight it was, too! Every day except Buddhist holidays, the boat with a long tail beeped its horn outside the house, and not only was it filled with every imaginable part of the pig, it also had a colorful vast array of noodles, sauces, herbs and condiments for sale.

SWEET AND SOUR PORK
Moo Pad Preaw Wan

Sweet and sour pork Thai style has lots of crispy vegetables and is not as sweet as its Chinese cousin.

4 to 6 servings

4 or 5 garlic cloves, finely chopped
¼ cup vegetable oil
2 pounds pork loin, cut into ½-inch chunks
2 medium cucumbers, peeled, halved lengthwise and thinly sliced
3 medium tomatoes, halved and thinly sliced
1 large onion, cut into ½-inch chunks
½ cup fish sauce
½ cup white vinegar
¼ cup sugar
1 teaspoon coarsely ground black pepper
2 tablespoons arrowroot powder
2 scallions, sliced into ½-inch pieces

In a wok or large frying pan, cook the garlic in the oil until it is light brown. Over high heat, stir in the pork and cook for 6 to 8 minutes. Add the cucumbers, tomatoes, onion, fish sauce, vinegar, sugar and black pepper. Lower the heat and simmer for 5 to 7 minutes. While the pork and vegetables simmer, dissolve the arrowroot in ¼ cup of hot water. Slowly add the dissolved arrowroot to the pork and continue stirring until the mixture has thickened slightly. Simmer for another 5 to 7 minutes, or until the pork is thoroughly cooked. Serve with rice and garnish with scallions.

GROUND PORK WITH GINGER
Nam Sod

A popular dish, Nam Sod is usually served as a light meal with rice, or as a snack.

4 to 6 servings

2 pounds ground pork
¼ cup julienned fresh ginger
¾ cup lemon juice
½ cup fish sauce
1 medium onion, halved and thinly sliced
3 coriander stems with roots, finely chopped
2 teaspoon crushed red pepper
1 large tomato, sliced into wedges
1 cucumber, thinly sliced
½ cup unsalted peanuts
Coriander leaves for garnish

In a wok or large frying pan, fry the ground pork with the ginger over medium heat for 5 minutes. Add the lemon juice and fish sauce and continue cooking for 3 to 5 minutes, or until the pork is no longer pink. Add the sliced onion, coriander and crushed red pepper. Reduce the heat and simmer for another 2 to 3 minutes, stirring to mix well. Serve on a platter, surrounded by tomato wedges and cucumber slices. Top with the peanuts and garnish with coriander leaves.

SWEET PORK
Moo Wan

The salty taste of Shrimp Paste Fried Rice (page 50) is a delicious contrast to the sweetness of Moo Wan.

4 to 6 servings

¼ cup vegetable oil
2 pounds pork loin, cut into 1-inch strips
¾ cup palm sugar or light brown sugar
1½ tablespoons black soy sauce
1 teaspoon light soy sauce
1 teaspoon coarsely ground black pepper

In a large wok or frying pan over high heat, heat the oil until it smokes. Add the pork strips and stir-fry for 3 minutes. Add the remaining ingredients. Lower the heat and simmer until the sauce is slightly thick and sticky, about 20 to 25 minutes.

PORK AND WATERCRESS IN CURRY
Kang Moo Te-Po

4 to 6 servings

¼ cup tamarind fruit or thawed frozen pulp
1½ cups unsweetened coconut milk
1½ tablespoons Red Curry Paste (page 22)
2 pounds pork loin, sliced into 1-inch strips
¼ cup fish sauce
2 tablespoons sugar
3 bunches watercress

Soak the tamarind in ½ cup of cold water for 1 hour. Discard the pulp and reserve the liquid. (If using tamarind syrup, omit this step and use only 1 tablespoon of sugar.)

In a large saucepan, heat ½ cup of coconut milk with the red curry paste. Stir for 3 minutes, or until the mixture is dark amber in color. Add the pork and coat thoroughly. Continue cooking over medium heat for 5 minutes. Add the remaining coconut milk, fish sauce, tamarind liquid and sugar. Stir well to mix the ingredients. Cover and simmer over low heat for 15 minutes, or until the pork is no longer pink and is completely cooked. Uncover, fold in the watercress, cook for another 2 to 3 minutes and serve.

SAUTEED PORK WITH SHRIMP PASTE
Moo Pad Kapi

4 to 6 servings

¼ cup vegetable oil
2 tablespoons shrimp paste
5 or 6 garlic cloves, finely chopped
2½ pounds pork loin, cut into 1-inch strips
2 tablespoons sugar
½ cup finely chopped shallots
3 fresh green chili peppers, seeded and thinly sliced on the diagonal
Coriander leaves for garnish

In a wok or large frying pan, heat the oil and stir-fry the shrimp paste and garlic over high heat for 2 minutes. Lower the heat to medium, add the pork and continue to stir-fry for 8 to 10 minutes, or until the pork is no longer pink. Add the sugar and shallots. Cook for another 3 minutes, mixing well. Fold in the chili peppers, garnish with coriander leaves and serve.

PORK IN HERB SAUCE
Moo Pa-Ro

All of the kids in my family loved this dish, so my mother always made enough to last a week. That last bowl of Moo Pa-Ro was the best, too, because each time it was reheated the flavor intensified, becoming sweeter and spicier. The special ingredient that made this dish so delicious was a blend of several spices called five-spice powder.

4 to 6 servings

7 or 8 garlic cloves
5 or 6 coriander stems with roots
1 teaspoon black peppercorns
¼ cup vegetable oil
2 pounds pork loin, cut into 1-inch chunks
1½ tablespoons five-spice powder
6 hard-cooked eggs, peeled
¼ cup sugar
2 tablespoons black soy sauce
½ cup fish sauce
4 bean curd cakes (about 16 ounces), cut into 1-inch cubes
Coriander leaves for garnish

Put the garlic cloves, coriander stems and peppercorns in a mortar with a pestle or in a food processor and mash them. In a wok or Dutch oven, heat the oil until it begins to smoke and add the garlic mixture. Reduce the heat and cook for 3 minutes. Raise the heat and add the pork chunks and five-spice powder, stirring to coat. Cook, stirring occasionally, for 7 to 8 minutes. Add enough cold water to cover the pork, and continue cooking until the liquid begins to boil.

Reduce the heat and add the hard-cooked eggs, sugar, black soy sauce and fish sauce. Simmer for 10 minutes. Add the bean curd, cover and continue simmering for 15 to 20 minutes. Add more water if needed to maintain a thick gravy-like consistency. Serve in a large bowl, garnished with coriander leaves and accompanied by rice. Moo Pa-Ro can be reheated many times; just add more hard-cooked eggs and more water for the gravy.

SAUTEED SPARERIBS WITH ONIONS AND PEPPER
Kra Dook Moo Tod

Thai men love spareribs, and my brothers could eat them by the pound! Of course, spareribs were eaten only at home, because my brothers insisted on staying "neat" when going out on the town, or, in our case, the village.

This is my mother's very delicious and very easy recipe. My husband, George, loves it for snacks, too.

4 to 6 servings

½ cup vegetable oil
4 pounds spareribs, cut into 1½- inch to 2-inch pieces (ask your
    butcher to cut them for you)
1 large onion, finely chopped
1½ tablespoons cracked black peppercorns
½ cup sugar
½ cup fish sauce
2 tablespoons black soy sauce

In a wok or large deep frying pan, heat the oil until it smokes. Add the spareribs and stir-fry until they are crisp, about 15 minutes. With a slotted spoon remove the spareribs from the wok and set aside on a platter. Discard all but 2 tablespoons of the oil.

Add the onion to the remaining oil and saute until light brown. Add the pepper, sugar, fish sauce and black soy sauce. Continue cooking until the sauce is blended and somewhat sticky, about 6 to 8 minutes. Add the spareribs, cook for another 5 minutes, toss them in the sauce until they are completely coated and serve.

ROAST PORK WITH RED GRAVY
Moo Dang

4 to 6 servings

2 teaspoons five-spice powder
¼ cup sesame oil
One 2½- to 3-pound boneless pork roast
¼ cup tomato paste
¼ cup sugar
1½ cups Thai Chicken Broth (page 34) or chicken stock
¼ cup fish sauce
2 tablespoons light soy sauce
2 tablespoons arrowroot
2 tablespoons sesame seeds
1 large cucumber, peeled and thinly sliced
2 scallions, chopped
Coriander leaves for garnish

Preheat the oven to 350° F. In a deep, flameproof covered baking dish or Dutch oven, cook the five-spice powder in the sesame oil for 3 minutes, stirring to blend. Add the pork roast and brown on all sides. Stir in the tomato paste and sugar. Add 1½ cups of cold water. Cover and place in the oven for 1 to 1½ hours, or until the pork is cooked (approximately 30 minutes per pound). Remove from the oven, raise the heat to broil and place under the broiler for 5 minutes so a light crust forms on top of the roast. Remove the roast from the baking dish and set aside while preparing the gravy.

Over medium heat, deglaze the baking dish with chicken stock, stirring constantly. Add the fish sauce and soy sauce and cook, stirring, for another 5 minutes. Remove ¼ cup of the simmering gravy and put in a small bowl. Dissolve the arrowroot in it and stir it slowly back into the gravy. Simmer for 8 to 10 minutes, or until the gravy has thickened slightly. Add the sesame seeds.

Thinly slice the pork roast and arrange on a large platter, covered with the cucumber slices. Pour the gravy on top, sprinkle with the chopped scallions and garnish with coriander leaves.

SAUTEED PORK WITH BASIL AND CHILI PEPPERS
Moo Pad Bai Kra Pow

Bai kra prow is Oriental basil and should not be confused with its Western cousin, sweet basil. Also called holy basil, it is available in Oriental groceries. If you cannot find it, substitute fresh mint leaves.

4 to 6 servings

6 or 7 garlic cloves, chopped
¼ cup vegetable oil
2 fresh green chili peppers, seeded and finely chopped
2½ pounds ground pork
½ cup sugar
¼ cup fish sauce
¼ cup black soy sauce
¼ cup chopped fresh Oriental basil leaves
4 or 5 whole Oriental basil leaves for garnish

In a wok or large frying pan, stir-fry the garlic in oil until light brown. Add the chopped chili peppers and stir-fry for 3 to 4 minutes. Add the ground pork and continue stir-frying for another 8 to 10 minutes. Add the sugar, fish sauce, black soy sauce and chopped basil, stirring constantly until the pork is completely cooked, about 5 minutes. Garnish with whole basil leaves and serve.

SAUTEED PORK WITH RED CURRY
Moo Pad Prik Keeng

4 to 6 servings

¼ cup vegetable oil
1½ tablespoons Red Curry Paste (page 22)
2 pounds pork loin, sliced into 1-inch strips
3 or 4 lemon leaves, crushed, or 1½ teaspoons grated lemon zest
1½ cups string beans
¼ cup fish sauce
¼ cup sugar

In a wok or large frying pan, heat the oil with the red curry paste. Mix well, add 2 tablespoons of cold water, the pork and lemon leaves and stir-fry for another 8 to 10 minutes, or until the pork is no longer pink and is completely cooked. Stir in the string beans, fish sauce, sugar and add ⅓ cup cold water. Cover and simmer over medium heat for 10 minutes. Serve with rice.

BEEF
Nuea

Like the pork boat, the beef boat would pass by our house every day on its way to the floating market. Once a week, as a courtesy to my mother, the vendor would stop at our house and the traditional haggling would begin. These weekly sessions would inevitably conclude with the beef vendor vowing never to return to our house and my mother swearing she had been robbed by paying his inflated prices. This went on for years, and we always had the best beef, not to mention the best entertainment.

Some of the beef she bought would be dried in the backyard under nets to protect it from bugs and small animals. I've never tasted anything that compares with my mother's spicy sun-dried beef.

Most of the recipes in this chapter call for boneless cuts; I use round steak or flank steak, but any boneless cut such as beef tenderloin or sirloin will work just as well.

꧋ꧏ꧋ꧏ꧋ꧏ꧋ꧏ꧋ꧏ꧋ꧏ꧋ꧏ꧋ꧏ꧋ꧏ꧋ꧏ꧋ꧏ꧋ꧏ꧋ꧏ꧋ꧏ꧋ꧏ꧋ꧏ꧋ꧏ꧋ꧏ꧋ꧏ

DRIED BEEF
Nuea Sa-Wan

In my village there was no pollution, only a very hot sun. To dry it, we would lay the marinated beef out on a tray covered by a protective net for the entire day. If you can dry your beef in the sun, like this, all the better. If not, do it the way I do in New York—overnight in a warm oven.

4 to 6 servings

2 pounds round steak, sliced into paper-thin (⅛-inch) 2-inch squares
3 tablespoons crushed coriander seeds
½ cup fish sauce
½ cup sugar
2 cups vegetable oil

Combine the meat wih the coriander seeds, fish sauce and sugar. Marinate for 6 to 8 hours in the refrigerator.

Cover a long flat tray or baking sheet with aluminum foil and place the marinated meat on it in one layer. Do not overlap the pieces. If necessary, use two trays. Turn the oven on at the lowest possible temperature and place the tray in the oven for a minimum of 7 hours, or overnight.

Once the beef is dried, heat the oil in a large frying pan. When the oil begins to smoke, fry the dried beef for 2 to 3 minutes on each side, until crusty. Serve it hot or cold, with rice or as a snack. The beef will keep for 2 weeks in the refrigerator.

GINGER BEEF
Nuea Pad Keeng

When I was a small child the waterways were not protected by dams, as they are today. So every winter around December the canals would flood, covering our garden. My brothers and I would take out a small rowboat and that's how we would play in our backyard. Occasionally my mother would let us stay in the boat and eat our dinner in it. She would often give us small boxes of rice and Nuea Pad Keeng.

4 to 6 servings

½ cup vegetable oil
4 or 5 garlic cloves, chopped
2 pounds round or flank steak, sliced into ¼-inch-thick 1-inch strips
⅓ cup finely chopped fresh ginger
1 fresh red chili pepper, seeded and thinly sliced on the diagonal
2 tablespoons fish sauce
¼ cup black bean sauce
1 tablespoon white vinegar
1 tablespoon sugar
½ cup tree fungus, soaked for 15 minutes in cold water and drained
½ cup finely chopped onions
2 scallions, chopped

In a wok or large frying pan, heat the oil until it smokes and add the garlic. Stir-fry the garlic until it is light brown. Add the beef and continue stir-frying for 5 to 7 minutes, until the strips are browned on both sides. Add the ginger and cook for another 2 to 3 minutes. Add the remaining ingredients, raise the heat to high and stir-fry for 5 to 7 minutes, or until the meat is cooked to taste. Serve with rice.

CHILI BEEF
Nuea Pad Prik

Here's a typical dinner dish, spicy-hot and colorful!

4 to 6 servings

⅓ cup vegetable oil
5 or 6 garlic cloves, finely chopped
2 pounds round or flank steak, sliced into ¼-inch-thick 1-inch strips
2 fresh red chili peppers, seeded and thinly sliced on the diagonal
2 fresh green chili peppers, seeded and thinly sliced on the diagonal
¾ cup coarsely chopped onions
½ cup fish sauce
1 tablespoon sugar
¼ cup coarsely chopped fresh Oriental basil leaves or fresh mint
    leaves

In a wok or large frying pan, heat the oil and stir-fry the garlic until it is light brown. Add the meat and stir-fry for 5 minutes, until the strips are browned. Add the chili peppers, onions, fish sauce and sugar. Continue stir-frying for another 8 to 10 minutes, or until the beef is cooked to taste and all of the ingredients are well mixed. Toss in the basil leaves and serve with rice.

GROUND BEEF SALAD
Lap Nuea

*Ground beef salad is usually served hot or cold at lunch with raw
vegetables such as lettuce, cucumbers and tomatoes.*

4 to 6 servings

1 tablespoon uncooked rice
2 tablespoons vegetable oil
4 or 5 garlic cloves, finely chopped
2½ pounds lean ground beef
1 cup lemon juice
½ cup fish sauce
1 medium onion, coarsely chopped
3 scallions, chopped
1 tablespoon crushed red pepper
1 small head crisp lettuce (romaine or iceberg)
1 large tomato, cut into wedges
1 cucumber, peeled and thinly sliced

In a small dry frying pan, toast the uncooked rice for 3 to 5 minutes,
or until the grains turn light brown. Remove the rice to a mortar with
a pestle or in a food processor and crush to a powder. Set aside.

In a wok or large frying pan, heat the oil and add the garlic, stir-
frying until it is light brown. Add the ground beef and stir-fry until
the meat loses its color, about 7 to 10 minutes. Stir in the lemon juice,
fish sauce and onion. Reduce the heat and simmer for 2 to 3 minutes
to blend the flavors. Remove the chopped beef mixture from the heat
and stir in the crushed rice, scallions and crushed red pepper. When
ready to serve, arrange the lettuce on a large platter, top with the
ground beef mixture and surround with the tomatoes and cucumber
slices.

BEEF PANANG CURRY
Panang Nuea

Beef panang is a very popular kaeng, or curry dish. It is usually served fiery hot, with the chili peppers cooked into the curry. I recommend adding the chili peppers to taste just before serving.

4 to 6 servings

1½ cups unsweetened coconut milk
1½ tablespoons Panang Curry Paste (page 24)
2½ pounds round or flank steak, sliced into ¼-inch-thick 1-inch
    strips
2 tablespoons fish sauce
2 tablespoons sugar
3 dried lemon leaves, crushed, or 1 tablespoon grated lemon zest
2 fresh green chili peppers, seeded and thinly sliced on the diagonal

In a large saucepan, heat ¼ cup of the coconut milk with the curry paste. Stir until blended into a deep amber liquid. Add the meat and cook, uncovered, over medium heat for 5 to 7 minutes. Stir in the fish sauce, sugar, lemon leaves and remaining coconut milk. Cover and simmer for 10 to 15 minutes, until the meat is cooked. Remove from the heat, stir in the chili peppers and serve with rice.

BEEF MASAMAN CURRY
Masaman Nuea

Beef masaman is a thick, stew-like kaeng, very mild, with a slightly sweet taste.

4 to 6 servings

¼ cup tamarind pulp, fresh, dried or frozen (thawed, if frozen)
1½ tablespoons Masaman Curry Paste (page 23)
3 cups unsweetened coconut milk
2 pounds round steak or stewing beef, cut into bite-size chunks
2 cups raw potatoes, peeled and diced
2 tablespoons fish sauce
½ cup shelled unsalted peanuts
2 tablespoons sugar
1 medium onion, coarsely chopped

Soak the tamarind pulp in ½ cup of cold water for 30 minutes. Discard the pulp, reserving the liquid. Set aside until ready to use. (If using tamarind syrup, omit this step and reduce the amount of sugar to 1 tablespoon.)

In a large pot, mix the masaman curry paste with 1 cup of coconut milk and simmer until the liquid is dark amber. Add the beef chunks and continue simmering for 8 to 10 minutes. Add the rest of the coconut milk and the remaining ingredients. Cover and simmer for 15 to 20 minutes, or until the meat is tender and the potatoes are cooked. Serve with rice.

BEEF SALAD
Nuea Nom Thok

Nuea Nam Thok is traditionally eaten as a snack food with alcoholic beverages, much like pretzels with beer. It was served in our household with kra-tche, a rice brew my mother was renowned for. Beef salad makes a wonderful lunch dish, too.

4 to 6 servings

2½ pounds round steak
1 cup lemon juice
½ cup fish sauce
½ cup finely chopped shallots
3 coriander stems with roots, finely chopped
2 scallions, chopped
¼ cup uncooked rice
½ tablespoon crushed red pepper
1 small head crisp lettuce (iceberg or romaine)
l large tomato, cut into wedges
1 cucumber, peeled and thinly sliced
Coriander leaves for garnish

Broil the meat until medium rare, about 7 to 10 minutes per side. Slice the steak into thin strips approximately 1 inch in length. Put the beef strips in a large bowl and add the lemon juice, fish sauce, shallots, coriander and scallions.

In a small dry frying pan, toast the rice until the grains turn light brown. Put the rice in a mortar with a pestle or in a food processor and crush the toasted grains. Add to the beef mixture. Stir in the crushed red pepper. When ready to serve, arrange the lettuce on a large platter. Top with the beef mixture and surround with the tomato wedges and cucumber slices. Garnish with coriander leaves.

BEEF IN RED CURRY
Kaeng Nuea

A family staple—there was almost always a pot of this cooking on the stove.

4 to 6 servings

1 tablespoon Red Curry Paste (page 22)
3 cups unsweetened coconut milk
2½ pounds round or flank steak, sliced into ¼-inch-thick 1-inch
    strips
2 to 3 lemon leaves, crushed, or 1½ teaspoons grated lemon zest
½ cup fish sauce
2 teaspoons sugar
½ cup bamboo shoots
½ cup peas, fresh or frozen (if frozen, thawed)
2 fresh green chili peppers, seeded and thinly sliced on the diagonal
5 fresh sweet basil leaves, coarsely chopped (optional)

In a large pot over low heat, stir the red curry paste into 1 cup of coconut milk. Cook until a thin layer of oil coats the surface. Add the meat and simmer over medium heat for 5 to 7 minutes. Add the rest of the coconut milk, lemon leaves, fish sauce, sugar, bamboo shoots and peas. Cover and simmer for 10 minutes, or until the beef is completely cooked. Stir in the chili peppers and sweet basil and cook for another 3 to 5 minutes. Serve with rice.

BEEF IN OYSTER SAUCE
Nuea Pad Pak Nam-Mon Hoi

4 to 6 servings

½ cup dried mushrooms
½ cup vegetable oil
4 or 5 garlic cloves, finely chopped
2 pounds round steak, sliced into ¼-inch-thick 1½- to 2-inch strips
1 cup broccoli, cut into bite-size pieces
1 large zucchini, sliced lengthwise, then cut into thin slices
2 or 3 bok choy stems, sliced into 2-inch pieces
¼ cup chopped walnuts
½ cup oyster sauce
2 tablespoons fish sauce
1 fresh red chili pepper, seeded and thinly sliced on the diagonal
2 tablespoons sugar
2 scallions, chopped

Soak the dried mushrooms in 1 cup of cold water for 30 minutes, or until softened. Drain and set aside. In a wok or large frying pan, heat the oil and stir-fry the garlic until it is light brown. Add the beef and stir-fry over high heat for 5 to 7 minutes, or until it loses its color. Add the broccoli, zucchini and bok choy and continue to stir-fry for 2 to 3 minutes. Add the walnuts, oyster sauce, fish sauce, chili pepper, sugar and ¼ cup of cold water. Reduce the heat to medium and continue cooking until the beef and vegetables are tender, about 5 to 7 minutes. Remove from the heat, stir in the chopped scallions and serve with rice.

SEAFOOD
Tat-Le

Where I grew up fish was a major part of the diet, and we caught our own fish because we lived on a canal, where fishing out the window was easy. Thai people fish from the shore by throwing nets into the water and having children go and retrieve the fish.

My brothers and sisters and I developed a method of retrieving the fish that was the quickest in the village. Since there were so many of us, we would form a line like a bucket brigade and throw the fish up to the shore; the last one to catch it would toss it into the fishing basket. All of this assembly-line action would stop, though, when we came across the dreaded pla-duc, *a local species of fish with poisonous fangs that also happens to be delicous when smoked. Only my father knew how to carefully pull it out of the net, so we would patiently wait on the shore while he dramatically extricated it.*

At the end of the day, the family would triumphantly return home with plenty of fish to bring to my mother, who was the quickest fish cleaner I have ever seen.

SEAFOOD WITH BASIL
Homok Tat-Le

When I was a student in Bangkok, I used to participate in an underground lottery with my friends. Whenever one of us would win, we would celebrate with a big seafood meal, like Homok Tat-Le.

4 to 6 servings

10 to 12 littleneck or cherrystone clams in the shell, cleaned
15 to 20 mussels in the shell, cleaned and rinsed several times to
  remove sand
½ pound raw squid, cleaned and sliced across into ½-inch pieces
1½ tablespoons Red Curry Paste (page 22)
2 tablespoons vegetable oil
1½ cups cold milk
1 tablespoon sugar
1 tablespoon fish sauce
¾ pound small shrimp, shelled and deveined
½ pound crabmeat, torn into bite-size pieces
½ pound scallops
½ pound red snapper or sea bass fillets, cut across into 2-inch pieces
7 or 8 celery cabbage (Napa cabbage) leaves
2 small bunches fresh sweet basil leaves (about 20 leaves)
2 fresh red chili peppers, seeded and thinly sliced on the diagonal

Preheat the oven to 350° F. Fill a large pot half full with water and bring to a boil. Add the clams, mussels and squid and return to a boil for 2 to 3 minutes, or until the clam and mussel shells open and the squid turns opaque white. Remove the seafood from the boiling water and rinse under cold water. Discard the shells from the clams and mussels and set the seafood aside.

In a large saucepan, heat the curry paste and vegetable oil over low heat for 2 to 3 minutes. Stir in the milk, sugar and fish sauce. Raise the heat to high and scald the milk. Remove from the heat and add the shrimp, crabmeat, scallops, fish fillets, clams, mussels and squid.

Line a deep casserole dish with a large sheet of aluminum foil, leaving enough extra foil to loosely fold over the top. Line the foil on the bottom and sides with the cabbage leaves. Pour in the fish mixture and carefully fold in basil leaves. Place the chili peppers on top of the mixture. Pinch the top of the foil closed and bake for 20 minutes. Serve with rice.

THAI BOUILLABAISSE
Po-Tak

4 to 6 servings

5 cups Thai Chicken Broth (page 34) or chicken stock
½ cup fish sauce
½ cup lemon sauce
2 or 3 lemon leaves, crushed, or 2 teaspoons grated lemon zest
1 tablespoon lemon grass (about 10 pieces dried lemon grass)
1 teaspoon crushed red pepper
15 to 20 mussels, cleaned and rinsed several times to remove sand
12 to 15 clams, cleaned
2 crab legs or claws in the shell, broken into bite-size pieces
½ pound red snapper or sea trout fillets, cut across into 2-inch-wide pieces
½ pound shrimp, cleaned
2 coriander stems with roots, coarsely chopped
Coriander leaves for garnish

In a large pot, boil the chicken stock, fish sauce, lemon juice, lemon leaves and lemon grass for 5 to 7 minutes. Add the crushed red pepper and remove from the heat. In a large heavy pot with a tight cover, layer the seafood, from the bottom, in the following order: mussels, clams, crab, red snapper or sea trout and shrimp. Sprinkle evenly with the chopped coriander. Pour the hot stock over the layered seafood and cover the pot. Simmer over medium heat for 3 to 5 minutes. Garnish with coriander leaves and serve.

FISH CAKES
Tod Man

When my father caught the big fish called pla-tchon, *it usually meant we would have fish cakes that night. Since my mother liked them very spicy, it also meant I was put to work grinding herbs in the khrok to make the curry paste.*

4 to 6 servings

2 pounds kingfish or bluefish fillets
1½ tablespoons Red Curry Paste (page 22)
1 tablespoon fish sauce
2 tablespoons arrowroot
1 tablespoon sugar
1 egg, beaten
2 or 3 lemon leaves, crushed, or 2 teaspoons grated lemon zest
1 cup string beans, chopped into ¼-inch pieces
2 cups vegetable oil

In a food processor, grind the fish to a pastelike consistency. (You can have it ground at your local fish market.) Place in a large bowl. Add the red curry paste, fish sauce, arrowroot, sugar, egg and lemon leaves. Refrigerate for 30 minutes for easier handling.

When ready to fry, add the string beans and form into 3-inch patties, about ¼ to ½ inch thick. Heat the oil until it smokes and fry the fish cakes until brown, about 7 minutes on each side. Serve them with the dipping sauce and rice.

DIPPING SAUCE
Nam Pla
1 small onion, coarsely chopped
½ teaspoon salt
¼ cup sugar
2 tablespoons coarsely chopped preserved garlic
1 tablespoon juice from preserved garlic jar
1 fresh red chili pepper, seeded and coarsely chopped
¼ cup white vinegar
1 large cucumber, peeled, seeded and coarsely chopped
½ cup ground unsalted peanuts

In a saucepan, mix the onion, salt, sugar, preserved garlic and juice, chili pepper and vinegar with 1 cup of cold water. Simmer, uncovered, over medium heat for 15 minutes. Remove from the heat and let cool for ½ hour. With a slotted spoon, separate the solid ingredients from the liquid and grind the solids with a mortar and pestle or in a food processor. Return the liquid to the saucepan, add the ground or blended solids and simmer, stirring constantly, for 8 to 10 minutes, to thicken.

When ready to serve the fish cakes, place the sauce in individual serving bowls with a tablespoon of the chopped cucumber and a teaspoon of the ground peanuts. Any leftover sauce can be refrigerated and stored for 2 months. The sauce may be served warm or cold.

DEEP-FRIED FISH IN SPICY-SWEET SAUCE
Pla Lad Prik

The sauce for this dish may be prepared in advance and will keep in the refrigerator for 2 weeks.

4 to 6 servings

¼ cup tamarind pulp, fresh, dried or frozen (if frozen, thawed)
½ tablespoon Red Curry Paste (page 22)
1 cup unsweetened coconut milk
2 tablespoons sugar
¼ cup fish sauce
2 or 3 lemon leaves, crushed, or 2 teaspoons lemon zest
Two 2-pound whole sea bass or red snappers, cleaned and scaled
½ cup all-purpose flour
2 cups vegetable oil
1 fresh red or green chili pepper, seeded and thinly sliced on the
     diagonal
Coriander leaves for garnish

Soak the tamarind pulp in ½ cup of cold water for 30 minutes. Discard the pulp and reserve the liquid. (If using bottled tamarind syrup, omit this step and reduce the amount of sugar to 1 tablespoon.) In a saucepan, heat the red curry paste and coconut milk over low heat until a thin layer of oil appears on the surface. Add the sugar, fish sauce, tamarind liquid and lemon leaves. Continue simmering over low heat while preparing the fish.

Make 4 shallow diagonal cuts in the skin of the fish on both sides to prevent curling. Dredge the fish in the flour. In a large frying pan, heat the oil until it smokes and fry the fish until it is golden brown and crisp, about 6 to 8 minutes per side. When ready to serve, arrange the fish on a platter, add the chili peppers to the simmering sauce and pour the sauce over the fish. Garnish with coriander leaves.

DEEP-FRIED FISH IN
TANGY GINGER SAUCE
Pla Gian

4 to 6 servings

2 cups plus 1 tablespoon vegetable oil
2 tablespoons black bean sauce
2 celery stalks, coarsely chopped
¼ pound mushrooms, sliced
¼ cup finely chopped fresh ginger
1 tablespoon fish sauce
1 cup Thai Chicken Broth (page 34) or chicken stock
1 fresh red chili pepper, seeded and thinly sliced on the diagonal
1 tablespoon sugar
1 tablespoon white vinegar
2 tablespoons arrowroot, dissolved in ¼ cup hot water
Two 2-pound whole sea bass or red snappers, cleaned and scaled
½ cup flour
½ teaspoon coarsely ground black pepper
Coriander leaves for garnish

In a large frying pan or wok, heat 1 tablespoon of oil and cook the black bean sauce for 2 to 3 minutes. Add the celery, mushrooms, ginger and fish sauce and stir-fry for 2 to 3 minutes, coating all of the ingredients. Stir in the chicken stock, chili pepper, sugar, vinegar and dissolved arrowroot. When the sauce begins to boil, reduce the heat and continue simmering while preparing the fish.

Make 4 shallow diagonal cuts on both sides of the fish to prevent curling. Dredge the fish in the flour. Heat the remaining 2 cups of oil in another deep frying pan until it begins to smoke. Fry the fish until it is golden brown, about 6 to 8 minutes on each side. Arrange the fish on a platter, pour the simmering sauce on top, sprinkle with black pepper and garnish with coriander leaves.

STUFFED SQUID IN RED SAUCE
Pla-Mook Sod-Sai Nam-Dang

4 to 6 servings

STUFFING
¾ pound ground pork
½ cup coarsely chopped bamboo shoots
¼ cup coarsely chopped water chesnuts
1 teaspoon ground black pepper
1 teaspoon finely chopped garlic
1 coriander stem with root, finely chopped
½ teaspoon sugar
2 tablespoons fish sauce
12 whole squid, cleaned, with cavities intact

SAUCE
3 tablespoons butter or margarine
¼ cup tomato sauce
½ cup dry red wine
¼ cup black soy sauce
1 tablespoon sugar
1 teaspoon ground black pepper

In a large mixing bowl, combine the ground pork, bamboo shoots, water chestnuts, black pepper, garlic, coriander, sugar and fish sauce. Refrigerate for ½ hour. Stuff the raw squid with the pork mixture, so that they are puffed and cylindrical. Place the stuffed squid on a flat steamer or steam tray and steam for 8 to 10 minutes, or until the squid turns opaque white. Remove from the heat and set aside while preparing the sauce. Preheat the oven to 450° F.

In a saucepan, melt the butter or margarine over low heat. Add the tomato sauce, stirring to blend. Stir in the wine, black soy sauce, sugar and pepper. Bring to a boil and add 1 cup of water. Return to a simmer for 5 to 7 minutes. While the sauce is simmering, arrange the steamed squid in a single layer in a deep casserole dish. Pour the sauce over the squid and cover. Bake for 30 minutes. Serve with steamed rice.

The sauce may be prepared 1 day in advance.

CURRIED SHRIMP WITH PINEAPPLE
Kaeng-Khow Sapbhalot

This is a very popular dish in Thailand, where it is usually made with mussels. For special occasions, though, I like it with shrimp.

4 servings

2 tablespoons tamarind pulp, fresh or frozen (if frozen, thawed)
1½ tablespoons Red Curry Paste (page 22)
1½ cups unsweetened coconut milk
¼ cup fish sauce
2 tablespoons sugar
3 or 4 lemon leaves, crushed, or 2½ teaspoons grated lemon zest
2 cups fresh pineapple, cut into bite-size chunks
1½ pounds medium shrimp, shelled and deveined

Soak the tamarind in ¼ cup cold water for 30 minutes. Discard the pulp and reserve the liquid. (In this recipe ¼ cup white vinegar may be substituted for the tamarind liquid.)

In a large saucepan, heat the red curry paste with the coconut milk over medium heat, simmering until a thin coat of oil appears on the surface. Stir in the fish sauce, tamarind liquid, sugar and lemon leaves. Bring the sauce to a boil, then reduce the heat. Add the pineapple and simmer for 5 minutes. Add the shrimp and simmer until completely cooked, about 3 to 5 minutes. Serve with steamed rice.

SPICY SOUR SHRIMP STEW
Gang Som

*In the countryside of Thailand this dish is made with tiny river fish.
In New York I make it with shrimp. Either way, it's delicious.*

4 to 6 servings

¼ cup tamarind pulp, fresh, dried or frozen (if frozen, thawed)
7 dried red chili peppers
1½ pounds small shrimp, shelled and deveined
4 shallots, peeled
6 garlic cloves, peeled
1½ tablespoons shrimp paste
¼ cup fish sauce
½ cup lemon juice
2 tablespoons sugar
1 large white turnip, peeled and diced (approximately 1 cup)
1 cup bok choy stems and leaves (sliced into 2-inch pieces)
2 cups coarsely chopped celery cabbage (Napa)
1 cup string beans, cut into 1½- to 2-inch pieces

Soak the tamarind pulp in ½ cup cold water for 30 minutes. Discard
the pulp and reserve the liquid. Set aside until ready to use. (If using
tamarind syrup, omit this step and reduce the amount of sugar to 1
tablespoon.) Soak the dried chili peppers in 1 cup of cold water for 15
minutes to soften. Remove from the water and chop. Set aside.

In a large pot, boil 2 cups of water. Add the shrimp and continue
boiling for 2 to 3 minutes, or until the shrimp are cooked. Remove the
shrimp with a slotted spoon, reserving the liquid, to a mortar with a
pestle or a food processor. Mash together the chili peppers, shallots,
garlic and shrimp paste. Add 2 tablespoons of the liquid the shrimp
were cooked in. Add 2 cooked shrimp and grind to a thin paste, using
more of the shrimp liquid to maintain this consistency.

Stir the paste into the remaining liquid in the pot. Over low heat,
stir until the paste dissolves, then add the tamarind liquid, fish

sauce, lemon juice and sugar. When the broth begins to boil, add the turnip. Cover and simmer for 5 minutes. Add the bok choy, celery cabbage and string beans. Continue cooking, covered, for 7 to 8 minutes, or until all of the vegetables are tender. Remove from the heat, stir in the cooked shrimp and serve in large bowls, with rice on the side.

FISH IN RED CURRY
Shu-Shi Pla

4 servings

1 tablespoon Red Curry Paste (page 22)
1½ cups unsweetened coconut milk
3 or 4 lemon leaves, crushed, or 2 tablespoons grated lemon zest
¼ cup fish sauce
2 tablespoons sugar
2 pound sea bass, sea trout or red snapper fillets, cut across into 1½-
    inch pieces

In a large pot over medium heat, stir the red curry paste into ¼ cup of coconut milk. Heat until a thin coat of oil appears on the surface. Add the lemon leaves, fish sauce and sugar. Stir in the remaining coconut milk. When the sauce begins to boil, carefully place the cut fillets in the pot. Reduce the heat. Simmer the fillets in the sauce for 7 to 8 minutes, or until they are cooked and have become opaque. Before serving, gently stir once, being careful not to break the fillets apart. Serve with rice.

GINGER FISH STEW
Tom Som

My mother often makes a large pot of Tom Som, and it will stay on the stove for days. She simply adds more fish to the stock, making it richer and more flavorful each day.

4 to 6 servings

¼ cup tamarind pulp, fresh, dried or frozen (if frozen, thawed)
1 tablespoon shrimp paste
5 or 6 garlic cloves, peeled
4 or 5 shallots, peeled
1 teaspoon black peppercorns
3 coriander stems with roots
¼ cup finely chopped fresh ginger
¼ cup fish sauce
2 tablespoons sugar
2 pounds sea bass or red snapper fillets, cut into 2-inch pieces
2 scallions, chopped
Coriander leaves for garnish

Soak the tamarind pulp in ½ cup of cold water for 30 minutes. Discard the pulp and reserve the liquid. (If using tamarind syrup, omit this step and reduce the amount of sugar to 1 tablespoon.) Put the shrimp paste, garlic cloves, shallots, peppercorns and coriander into a mortar with a pestle or a food processor. Mash into a thick paste. In a large pot, boil 4 cups of water. Add the paste and stir until it is dissolved.

Stir in the ginger, fish sauce, sugar and tamarind liquid. Bring to a boil, then reduce the heat. Gently place the fish fillets in the pot. Add the scallions, but do not stir. Simmer for 8 to 10 minutes, or until the fish fillets are opaque and completely cooked. Serve in large individual bowls, garnished with coriander leaves.

STEAMED FISH
Pla Nuang

In the country we make our steamed fish dishes very spicy and very tart. I use pickled plums and the juice from the jar to add even more tartness. Pickled plums can be found in Oriental groceries.

4 servings

One 3-pound whole sea bass or white snapper, cleaned and scaled
3 pickled plums, coarsely chopped
¼ cup juice from the pickled plum jar
½ cup Thai Chicken Broth (page 34) or chicken stock
¼ teaspoon ground black pepper
¼ cup celery leaves
2 scallions, chopped
1 fresh red chili pepper, seeded and coarsely chopped

Make two slits in the skin across the width of the fish on both sides, to prevent curling. Place the fish in a fish poacher or a shallow pan with a cover. Sprinkle the chopped pickled plum on top of the fish. Add the plum juice, chicken stock and pepper. Cover and steam, over low heat, for 15 minutes.

Add the celery leaves, scallions and chopped chili pepper. Cover again and steam for another 5 to 7 minutes, or until the fish is completely cooked. Serve with rice.

NOODLES
Kuwae Tee-Ow
Leh Sen

In Thailand noodles are eaten at lunch with chopsticks. It is almost the only time we use chopsticks. Noodles are served with a soup or in the soup, as the main course. Most Thai noodle dishes are of Chinese origin and are usually stir-fried.

Thai noodles are usually made from rice flour or mung bean flour, and can be purchased in Oriental groceries. Like all types of dried noodles, they can be stored indefinitely.

RICE FLAKES WITH PORK
Sen Kuwae-Chap Pad Moo

4 to 6 servings

One 16-ounce package rice flakes
5 or 6 garlic cloves, finely chopped
¼ cup vegetable oil
2 fresh green chili peppers, seeded and thinly sliced on the diagonal
¼ cup white vinegar
1 tablespoon five-spice powder
1 pound boneless pork loin, cut into bite-size chunks
4 hard-cooked eggs, peeled
2 coriander stems with roots, finely chopped
2 tablespoons fish sauce
2 tablespoons black soy sauce
¼ cup sugar
2 firm-style bean curd cakes, cut into ½-inch cubes

In a large pot bring 10 cups of water to a boil. Add the rice flakes and boil for 10 minutes. Drain, rinse the rice flakes in cold water and set aside.

In a small skillet, saute the garlic in 2 tablespoons of oil until light brown. Pour the garlic and oil into a small bowl, to be used as a condiment. In another small bowl, mix the chili peppers and the vinegar. Set aside.

In a large pot, heat the remaining oil and stir in the five-spice powder. Add the pork, eggs and coriander. Cook over low heat for 5 minutes, stirring to coat all of the ingredients. Add 5 cups of water, raise the heat and bring to a boil. Stir in the fish sauce, black soy sauce and sugar. Add the bean curd, cover and simmer for 15 to 20 minutes, or until the pork is completely cooked.

Remove the eggs and slice into quarters. Return them to the pot. Add the noodles and cook for 5 minutes, stirring occasionally. Serve in a large bowl, accompanied by the small side bowls of garlic in oil and chili pepper in vinegar.

SAUTEED NOODLES IN BEAN SAUCE
Pad See-Um

4 to 6 servings

One 16-ounce package rice noodles
6 or 7 garlic cloves, coarsely chopped
¼ cup vegetable oil
1 pound pork loin, sliced into ¼-inch-thick 1-inch strips
1½ cups broccoli stems, peeled and cut diagonally into 1½-inch
    pieces
¼ cup white vinegar
1 tablespoon fish sauce
¼ cup black bean sauce
¼ cup black soy sauce
3 medium eggs
2 tablespoons sugar
½ teaspoon crushed red pepper
Coriander leaves for garnish

In a large bowl, soak the rice noodles in 10 to 12 cups of cold water
for 2 hours. Drain and cover with a wet towel to retain moisture.

In a wok or large frying pan, stir-fry the garlic in the oil until it is
light brown. Add the pork and cook for 5 minutes, coating well. Add
the broccoli stems and vinegar and stir-fry over high heat for 2 to 3
minutes. Reduce the heat to medium and add the noodles, fish sauce,
black bean sauce and black soy sauce. Continue stirring for 5 minutes. Push the ingredients to the side of the wok or frying pan,
creating a space in the middle. Crack the eggs into this space and
quickly stir, folding them into the noodle-pork mixture. Continue to
stir vigorously to combine all of the ingredients well. Add the sugar
and crushed red pepper and continue stirring over medium heat for 3
to 5 minutes. Garnish with coriander leaves and serve.

YELLOW NOODLES WITH BEEF CONSOMME
Kuwae Tee-ow Nuea

When I first moved to New York, I didn't know how to get to the shops that sold Oriental products. So, unless my husband or a friend was free to take me to Chinatown, I had to experiment with whatever was available in the neighborhood markets. For this dish I substituted packaged egg noodles, and they're excellent, but if you do have the opportunity to shop in an Oriental market, ask for fresh Chinese yellow noodles.

4 to 6 servings

1 pound fresh Chinese yellow noodles or one 16-ounce package (½-inch wide) egg noodles
5 or 6 garlic cloves, coarsely chopped
¼ cup vegetable oil
2 or 3 fresh green chili peppers, seeded and thinly sliced diagonally
¼ cup white vinegar
2 celery stalks, coarsely chopped
2 cinnamon sticks
2 to 3 star anise
3 coriander stems with roots, finely chopped
½ cup fish sauce
½ cup black soy sauce
¼ cup sugar
1½ pounds round steak, cut into 1½-inch chunks
½ pound calf's liver, sliced into 1-inch strips
½ teaspoon crushed red pepper
½ pound mung bean sprouts, soaked in hot water for 15 minutes and drained
Coriander leaves for garnish

If using fresh noodles, cook them in boiling water for no longer than 2 to 3 minutes. Drain thoroughly and set aside. If using packaged egg noodles, cook according to package directions, drain and set aside. Stir-fry the garlic in oil until light brown. Set aside. In a small dish marinate the chili peppers in the vinegar.

Fill a large pot with 10 to 12 cups of cold water, about three-quarters full. Add the celery, cinnamon sticks, star anise, coriander, fish sauce, black soy sauce and sugar. Cook over medium heat. When it begins to boil, add the beef chunks. Cover, reduce the heat and simmer for ½ hour, until the beef has cooked completely. Add the liver and crushed red pepper. Cover again and continue simmering for 5 to 7 minutes, or until the liver is no longer pink.

In large, individual bowls, put in a layer of bean sprouts, then top with the noodles. Ladle the consomme over the sprouts and noodles and add a generous portion of the meat. Float the stir-fried garlic on top, garnish with coriander leaves and serve with marinated chili peppers on the side.

SAUTEED RICE NOODLES
Pad Thai

Rice noodles look like long white fettuccine noodles and are available in 16-ounce packages.

4 servings

One 16-ounce package rice noodles
½ cup vegetable oil
5 or 6 garlic cloves, finely chopped
1 pound medium shrimp, shelled and deveined
2 firm-style bean curd squares, cut into ½-inch cubes
¼ cup coarsely chopped pickled turnips
½ cup white vinegar
¼ cup fish sauce
1 tablespoon paprika
¼ cup sugar
2 eggs, beaten
¼ pound mung bean sprouts
3 scallions, cut into ½-inch pieces
½ cup ground unsalted peanuts
1 fresh red chili pepper, seeded and coarsely chopped
1 lemon, cut into wedges
Coriander leaves for garnish
¼ cup crushed red pepper (optional)

In a large bowl, soak the rice noodles in 10 to 12 cups of cold water for 2 hours. Drain and cover with a damp towel to retain moisture.

In a wok or large frying pan, heat the oil and stir-fry the garlic until it is light brown. Add the shrimp, bean curd and pickled turnips; stir in the vinegar, fish sauce, paprika and sugar. When thoroughly mixed, fold in the noodles. When the noodles are completely coated, spread them out to the sides of the wok or frying pan, leaving a space in the middle. Add the beaten eggs. As the eggs cook, fold the noodles over them and stir to evenly combine all of the ingredients. Stir in half of the bean sprouts, then add the scallions, ground peanuts and chopped chili pepper. Toss several times to mix well.

Serve on a large platter with lemon wedges. Top with the remaining bean sprouts and garnish with coriander leaves. Serve the crushed red pepper on the side, for those who like it extra-spicy.

NOODLES WITH THAI CHICKEN SOUP
Kuwae Tee-ow Gai

At lunch, it is quite common in Thailand to serve a hearty soup as the main course. We serve it in individual portions, using large bowls and layering the ingredients, rather than cooking them all together.

4 to 6 servings

7 or 8 garlic cloves, coarsely chopped
½ cup vegetable oil
One 16-ounce package of rice flakes
One 3-pound whole chicken
1 celery stalk, coarsely chopped
3 coriander stems with roots, finely chopped
½ cup fish sauce
1 tablespoon sugar
½ cup coarsely chopped pickled turnips
¼ cup dried shrimp
¼ cup ground unsalted peanuts
1 teaspoon ground black pepper
2 eggs, beaten
½ pound mung bean sprouts, soaked in hot water for 15 minutes and
    drained
2 scallions, chopped
Coriander leaves for garnish

Stir-fry the garlic in ¼ cup of oil until light brown. Set aside. Soak the rice flakes in hot water for 20 minutes, drain and set aside.

Fill a large pot, three-quarters full with cold water—about 10 to 12 cups, depending upon the size of the pot. Add the chicken, celery, coriander, fish sauce and sugar. Bring the water to a boil, cover, reduce heat and simmer for 1 to 1½ hours. When the chicken has cooked completely and can easily be pulled off the bone, remove it from the pot. Add the pickled turnips, dried shrimp, ground peanuts and ground pepper. Simmer, uncovered, for 20 minutes. While these ingredients are cooking, remove the skin from the chicken and tear the meat off the bones. Set the chicken meat aside.

In a small frying pan, saute the eggs in the remaining oil to prepare an omelette. Tear it into bite-size chunks and set aside.

When ready to assemble the ingredients for the soup, layer from the bottom up in individual large soup bowls, as follows: 1½ tablespoons of mung bean sprouts, as the bottom layer; ¼ cup of the rice flakes; ¼ cup of the boned chicken; 2 tablespoons of the omelette chunks; 1 teaspoon of the stir-fried garlic; 1 cup of the broth, poured over the layers; ½ teaspoon chopped scallions, sprinkled on top. Garnish with the coriander leaves and serve. These amounts may be adjusted to suit personal preference, of course.

YELLOW NOODLES WITH ROAST PORK
Bah Mi Moo Dang

The roast pork can be prepared a day ahead of time.

4 to 6 servings

ROAST PORK
1½ teaspoons five-spice powder
2 tablespoons tomato paste
½ cup sugar
One 2½-pound boneless pork roast

In a large covered baking dish, combine the five-spice powder with the tomato paste, sugar and 2 cups of cold water. Place the pork roast in the marinade, turning several times to coat, and refrigerate, covered, for 2 to 4 hours.

Preheat the oven to 350° F. Roast the pork in the marinade for 1½ to 2 hours, or until the pork is completely cooked and no longer pink inside. Let the roast rest for 15 minutes, then slice thinly. Refrigerate until ready to use.

NOODLES AND BROTH
2 or 3 fresh green chili peppers, seeded and thinly sliced on the
    diagonal
¼ cup white vinegar
5 or 6 garlic cloves, finely chopped
¼ cup vegetable oil
1 cup bok choy sliced into 2-inch pieces
1 pound fresh yellow noodles or one 16-ounce package dried egg
    noodles
5 cups Thai Chicken Broth (page 34) or chicken stock
½ cup fish sauce
¼ cup sugar
1 teaspoon ground black pepper

3 scallions, chopped
½ cup ground unsalted peanuts
2 tablespoons crushed red pepper

In a small shallow bowl, marinate the chili peppers in the vinegar. Set aside. In a frying pan, stir-fry the garlic in the oil until it is light brown. Set aside in a small bowl. In a steamer, steam the bok choy until tender, about 7 to 8 minutes. Set aside. In a large pot, bring 10 cups of water to a boil and add the fresh noodles. Continue boiling for 2 to 3 minutes. Drain and set aside. (If using packaged egg noodles, prepare according to the directions.)

In a large pot over medium heat, mix the chicken stock, fish sauce, sugar and black pepper. Bring to a boil, reduce the heat and simmer until ready to use.

Place ¼ cup of the bok choy in each large individual soup bowl and top with ½ cup of the noodles and 4 or 5 slices of the roast pork. Fill the bowls with the simmering broth. Float the stir-fried garlic on top and sprinkle with scallions, ground peanuts and crushed red pepper to taste. Serve with the marinated chili peppers on the side.

STIR-FRIED BEAN THREADS
Pad Woon Sen

Woon sen noodles are made from mung bean flour and have a chewy, almost sticky texture. They are delicious stir-fried with vegetables or simmered in soups. Pad Woon Sen is a typical Thai lunch dish: stir-fried bean threads with vegetables. Variations of this dish with dried shrimp and ground pork are delicious.

4 servings

One 12-ounce package bean thread noodles or three 4-ounce
    packages
6 or 7 garlic cloves, finely chopped
½ cup vegetable oil
1 cup coarsely chopped celery cabbage (Napa cabbage) or green leaf
    (savoy) cabbage
¼ cup fish sauce
2 tablespoons sugar
2 large tomatoes, coarsely chopped
4 eggs, beaten
2 fresh red chili peppers, thinly sliced on the diagonal
3 scallions, chopped
Coriander leaves for garnish

Soak the bean thread noodles in cold water for 1 hour. Drain and set aside. In a wok or large frying pan, stir-fry the garlic in the oil until it is light brown. Add the cabbage and continue stir-frying, coating the cabbage with the garlic and oil. Add the fish sauce, sugar, tomatoes and soaked bean threads. Raise the heat to high and stir-fry for 3 to 5 minutes.

Spread the ingredients along the side of the wok or frying pan, creating a well in the middle. Add the eggs, and as they begin to cook, quickly fold the noodles over them, stirring to mix well. Stir in the chili peppers and scallions. Serve on a large platter and garnish with coriander leaves.

STIR- FRIED BEAN THREADS WITH DRIED SHRIMP
Phao Pad Woon Sen

Soak ½ cup of dried shrimp in cold water for 15 minutes. Drain the dried shrimp and add to the noodles, along with the chili peppers and scallions. Continue stir-frying for 2 to 3 minutes, until thoroughly mixed. Serve on a large platter, garnished with coriander leaves.

STIR-FRIED BEAN THREADS WITH PORK
Moo Pad Woon Sen

Add 1 pound of ground pork after the garlic is browned. Stir-fry for 3 to 5 minutes, or until the pork loses its pink color.

NOODLES WITH SHRIMP AND BROCCOLI
Pad Lad-Na Kung

For this dish we use fresh noodles, which can be found only in Chinese noodle shops. When I was a child, we would go to the floating market and buy them from an old Chinese woman who made them fresh daily. Now I buy them in Chinatown, where they are cut to order, like fresh Italian pasta.

If you don't live in an area with a Chinese market, prepare this dish with sen lek, or rice noodles. Remember to soak them in cold water for 2 hours before cooking.

4 to 6 servings

2 fresh green chili peppers, seeded and thinly sliced diagonally
¼ cup white vinegar
8 to 10 garlic cloves, finely chopped
¼ cup vegetable oil
2 cups peeled broccoli stems diagonally cut into 1-inch pieces
2 tablespoons black bean sauce
1 pound medium shrimp, shelled and deveined
5 cups Thai Chicken Broth (page 34) or chicken stock
¼ cup black soy sauce
1 tablespoon fish sauce
2 tablespoons sugar
2 tablespoons arrowroot
1 pound fresh Chinese noodles, cut 1 inch wide

Add the chili peppers to the vinegar. Set aside in a small bowl, to be served as a condiment. In a large pot, saute half of the garlic in 2 tablespoons of oil until it turns light brown. Add the broccoli stems and black bean sauce. Stir over medium heat for 3 minutes and add the shrimp. Saute the shrimp for 2 to 3 minutes and pour in the chicken stock, 2 tablespoons of black soy sauce, fish sauce and sugar.

In a small bowl, dissolve the arrowroot in ¼ cup of hot water.

Slowly stir it into the pot of soup. Raise the heat and bring to a boil. Remove from the heat, stirring occasionally while it thickens. In a wok or large frying pan, stir-fry the rest of the garlic in the remaining oil. Add the noodles and the rest of the black soy sauce and stir-fry over high heat for 5 to 7 minutes, or until they are completely coated with sauce and soft.

Put the noodles at the bottom of a large serving bowl or divide between individual soup bowls. Pour the broth with the vegetables and shrimp over them. Serve with the marinated chili peppers on the side.

RICE VERMICELLI SAUTEED WITH PORK
Mai Fun Pad Moo

Sen-mee noodles, also known as rice vermicelli, come in packages containing one or three bundles. They can be deep-fried directly out of the bag, as in Mee Krob (Fried Rice Sticks with Tamarind Sauce, see page 68), or soaked and sauteed, as in this recipe.

4 to 6 servings

One 3-bundle or 12-ounce bag rice vermicelli
4 or 5 garlic cloves, finely chopped
¼ cup vegetable oil
1 pound ground pork
¼ cup black bean sauce
¼ cup tomato paste
2 tablespoons fish sauce
¼ cup Thai Chicken Broth (page 34) or chicken stock
1 teaspoon ground black pepper
2 tablespoons sugar
½ pound small shrimp, shelled and deveined
3 scallions, chopped
2 teaspoons crushed red pepper
Coriander leaves for garnish

Soak the noodles in cold water for ½ hour. Drain and cover with a damp towel to retain moisture.

In a wok or large frying pan, stir-fry the garlic in the oil until it turns light brown. Add the pork, raise the heat to high, and stir-fry for 3 minutes. Stir in the black bean sauce, tomato paste, fish sauce, chicken stock, black pepper and sugar. Continue stir-frying for 5 to 7 minutes, or until the pork is completely cooked. Add the shrimp and stir-fry for 3 to 5 minutes, until cooked.

Fold in the noodles and toss to coat with the sauce and mix with all of the ingredients. Add the scallions and crushed red pepper. Serve on a large platter, garnished with coriander leaves.

DESSERTS
Kha-Nom

Thai desserts have a subtle sweetness and are usually prepared from grains, rice flour, mung bean flour and sweet rice (also known as glutinous rice). Since I have never been a great lover of desserts, I usually have to rely on the knowledgable sweet tooth of my husband, George.

Most of the following recipes are his favorites, or the traditional desserts served by my mother. The necessary ingredients for most of these recipes can be found only in Oriental groceries.

MUNG BEAN PASTRIES
Lum Klum

Approximately 2 dozen

½ cup mung bean flour
¾ cup sugar
2 or 3 drops red or green food coloring
¼ cup rice flour
¾ cup unsweetened coconut milk
½ teaspoon salt
2 tablespoons yellow mung beans, also known as peeled mung beans
   (optional)

In a large bowl, combine the mung bean flour, sugar, food coloring and 2 cups of cold water. Stir until the flour is almost dissolved. Strain the liquid through a double thickness of cheesecloth into a saucepan. Over medium heat, stir the liquid until any remaining solids are completely dissolved and the mixture has become thick and sticky enough to coat a spoon. Remove from the heat and allow to cool for 15 minutes, until barely warm.

Cover a baking sheet with waxed paper. Drop the mixture by tablespoonsful, onto the sheet, allowing enough space so the circles do not touch as they spread. While the gelatin cools to room temperature, prepare the topping. In a large bowl, combine the rice flour, coconut milk and salt, stirring until dissolved. Strain the mixture into a saucepan through a double thickness of cheesecloth. Cook over medium heat for 10 minutes, or until the mixture is thick enough to coat a spoon. Drop 1 teaspoonful of the rice flour mixture on top of each of the cooling gelatin circles.

In a dry skillet, toast the yellow mung beans until they turn light brown. Generously sprinkle on top of the pastries. Refrigerate for 1 hour before serving. The pastries will be thick enough to pick up and eat with your hands. They will keep in the refrigerator for 2 to 3 days.

THAI CUSTARD
Sung Kha Ya

Thai custard is prepared by steaming and is served either hot or cold. When served hot, it is usually over a steaming portion of Sweet Rice (page 137).

4 to 6 servings

5 large eggs
½ cup light brown sugar
1 cup unsweetened coconut milk

Beat the eggs, brown sugar and coconut milk until thoroughly mixed and frothy. The color will be a pale yellow. Pour the mixture into a shallow pan and steam on a steam tray or in a steamer for 30 to 35 minutes, or until the custard has set. To check, stick a toothpick into the center and see if it comes out clean. Time variations may occur with different steaming methods. Spoon into individual serving dishes while hot, or allow to cool and cut into squares.

PUMPKIN CUSTARD
Sung Kha Ya Fuchtong

This is probably one of the most popular variations of Thai custard. Again, serve it with or without sweet rice.

4 to 6 servings

5 large eggs
½ cup light brown sugar
1 cup unsweetened coconut milk
¼ cup fresh pumpkin, sliced into thin strips (about 2 inches long
    and ⅛ inch thick)

Beat the eggs, brown sugar and coconut milk until thoroughly mixed and frothy. The color will be a pale yellow. Pour the mixture into a shallow pan, and steam on a steam tray or in a steamer for 15 to 20 minutes, or until the custard is firm when gently touched at the surface.

Decoratively place the pumpkin strips on top of the custard. Resume steaming for 15 to 20 minutes, or until the entire custard has set. Serve hot in individual serving dishes or over sweet rice, or serve cold cut into squares.

SWEET RICE
Khow Neeow

Sweet rice is always served steaming hot or warm. Top each serving with custard or fruit, or serve it plain.

4 to 6 servings

1½ cups short-grain rice
1½ cups unsweetened coconut milk

Place the rice in a bowl with 2 cups of cold water. Cover the bowl and soak the rice overnight.

Thirty minutes to 1 hour before serving, place the rice and whatever water has not been absorbed into a medium-size pot. Stir in the coconut milk, cover tightly and cook over low heat for 20 minutes. After the first 10 minutes, stir once. The finished rice will have a thick, sticky consistency, with soft but not mushy grains.

SWEET RICE PUDDING WITH LONGAN FRUIT
Khow Neeow Lum-Yai

Longan fruit is very popular in Thailand. It looks very much like its cousin the lichee nut and grows on trees, in dark brown, round shells. The shells peel off easily, and only the white soft flesh is eaten. Outside of Thailand, I have found longan fruit only canned in syrup, which makes a totally suitable dessert, the fruity syrup actually enriching the dish. If longan fruit is not available in your area, substitute 1½ cups diced fresh coconut meat, and add ½ cup water and ¼ cup sugar to the recipe.

4 to 6 servings

1 cup short-grain rice
½ cup sugar
One 14-ounce can longan fruit in syrup
½ cup unsweetened coconut milk
½ teaspoon salt

Soak the rice in 2 cups of cold water for 20 minutes. Drain. Put the soaked rice in a large saucepan, add 3 cups of cold water and cook over medium heat, uncovered, for 30 minutes. Stir every 5 minutes to prevent the rice from sticking as the water evaporates. Stir in the sugar and cook for another 5 minutes.

Add the longan fruit with the syrup and cook for another 5 minutes. Cover and remove from the heat. In a small saucepan, heat the coconut milk and salt over low heat until it begins to boil. Remove from the heat and allow to cool for 10 minutes. Serve the pudding warm, with each serving topped with 1 tablespoon of the coconut milk.

BEAN CAKE WITH COCONUT MILK
Kha Nom Moa-Kang

4 to 6 servings

1 cup yellow mung beans
1½ cups unsweetened coconut milk
1 cup palm sugar or 1½ cups light brown sugar
6 large eggs, beaten
½ cup finely chopped shallots
3 tablespoons vegetable oil

In a medium-size pot, combine the mung beans with 1 cup of water and bring to a boil. Reduce the heat to low and cook for 10 minutes. Put the cooked beans in a mortar with pestle or a food processor and mash into a thick paste. In a bowl, beat the coconut milk and sugar until well blended and frothy. Add the eggs and mashed mung beans, and continue beating until thoroughly mixed. Put the mixture in a saucepan and stir over medium heat until the ingredients begin to thicken, about 10 minutes.

Preheat the oven to 350° F. Grease an 8-inch square cake pan and fold the mung bean mixture into it, smoothing the top with a spatula. Bake for 20 minutes, until the cake begins to turn deep yellow. Raise the heat to 450° F and bake for another 25 to 30 minutes, until the bean cake turns deep amber.

Remove from the oven and immediately immerse the cake pan in ½ inch of cold water for 10 minutes. Change the water continuously to ensure that it stays cold, and continue cooling this way for 15 minutes.

In a small pan, saute the shallots in the oil until light brown. Drain off the oil and spread the shallots over the top of the cake. When the cake has cooled to slightly warmer than room temperature, cut into squares and serve. Bean cake will keep for 1 week in the refrigerator and may be served warm or cold.

RICE BALLS IN COCONUT MILK
Kha Nom Bua-Loi

4 to 6 servings

1 cup rice flour
½ cup arrowroot
3 cups unsweetened coconut milk
1 cup sugar
½ teaspoon salt
½ teaspoon vanilla extract

Mix the rice flour, arrowroot and ¼ cup of cold water. Turn the mixture out onto a smooth surface and knead. It should have the consistency of piecrust dough. Add more water if necessary. With your hands, shape into 1½-inch balls.

Fill a large pot half full with water and bring to a boil. Drop the balls into the boiling water, four at a time, so they don't stick together. Boil for 4 to 5 minutes, or until they float to the top. Remove with a slotted spoon and repeat this process until all of the balls are cooked.

In a large saucepan, heat the coconut milk, sugar, salt and vanilla extract over medium heat for 5 to 7 minutes. Add the rice balls and continue cooking, stirring constantly, until the coconut milk begins to boil. Serve hot.

YELLOW MUNG BEAN PUDDING
Thao Suan

4 to 6 servings

1½ cups yellow mung beans
2 tablespoons arrowroot
1 cup sugar
¼ cup unsweetened coconut milk
¼ teaspoon salt

Soak the mung beans in 2 cups of cold water for 20 minutes. Drain and place in a large pot. Add 10 cups of cold water. Cook over medium heat, uncovered, for 15 minutes. Dissolve the arrowroot in ¼ cup of hot water and stir into the mung beans. Add the sugar and continue cooking, stirring occasionally, for 15 minutes, or until all of the water has been absorbed. Remove from the heat.

In a small saucepan, heat the coconut milk with the salt for 5 to 7 minutes, or until it begins to boil. Serve the pudding in individual bowls, topped with 1 tablespoon of the coconut milk. The pudding will keep in the refrigerator for 1 week, and may be served hot or cold.

MUNG BEANS WITH BROWN SUGAR
Tuea-Keow Tom Nam-Tan

This remarkable confection, with its soupy consistency and spicy flavor, is not only eaten as a dessert, but given to children with high fever as a delicious medicine. My mother insists that it can literally cool your insides—maybe because it is eaten so hot that anything else is cool by comparison.

4 to 6 servings

1½ cups dried whole mung beans
1 cup light brown sugar
1 tablespoon finely chopped fresh ginger

Soak the mung beans in 2 cups of cold water for 30 minutes. Remove any beans that float to the top. Drain. In a large pot, combine the soaked beans and 7 cups of water. Simmer, uncovered, over medium heat for 30 to 35 minutes. With a slotted spoon, remove any floating skins. Stir in the sugar and ginger. Cover, reduce the heat to low, and continue cooking for 15 minutes. Serve hot.

SWEET RICE CAKES STUFFED WITH YELLOW BEANS
Kha-Nom Tuea Pap

4 to 6 servings

½ cup yellow mung beans
2 cups unsweetened dried grated coconut
½ teaspoon salt
3 tablespoons white sesame seeds
¼ cup sugar
2 cups rice flour

Simmer the mung beans in 1 cup of cold water for 20 minutes. Drain and set aside. Mix the coconut with salt. Sprinkle evenly on a flat dish and set aside. In a small pan over low heat, toast the sesame seeds until light brown. Mix the toasted sesame seeds into the sugar, evenly spread on another flat dish and set aside.

In a large bowl, mix the rice flour with ½ cup of water and knead into a dough the consistency of piecrust dough. Mold the rice flour dough into 1½-inch balls, then flatten with the palm of your hand to form thin round cakes, about 2 inches wide and ⅛ inch thick. Fill a large pot half full with water and bring to a boil. Drop the rice flour cakes into the boiling water four to five at a time, so they don't stick together. Boil for 3 to 4 minutes, or until they float to the top.

While still hot, coat each side of the rice cakes with the coconut-salt mixture. Place ¼ to ½ teaspoon of the yellow mung beans in the middle of each cake. Fold the edges over and pinch closed to form a half circle. Dip each rice cake into the sesame seed–sugar mixture, coating both sides well. Serve hot or cold. Rice cakes will keep refrigerated, for 2 to 3 days.

BANANAS IN COCONUT MILK
Khrow Buad Chi

4 to 6 servings

2½ cups unsweetened coconut milk
¼ cup sugar
½ teaspoon salt
4 large bananas, peeled and diagonally sliced into 1½-inch pieces

In a large saucepan, bring the coconut milk to a boil. Add the sugar and salt, and cook for 3 to 5 minutes over medium heat. Reduce the heat, add the sliced bananas, cover and simmer for 5 minutes. Do not stir, or the bananas will become mushy. Serve hot or cold.

MENUS

Thai food lends an exotic flavor to any style of entertaining, whether you serve a traditional meal or integrate Thai dishes to add a festive feeling to a special occasion. Here are some of the menus I use for parties and gatherings.

Thai Feast for 6 to 8 People

This banquet is an excellent way to show off your Thai cooking skills to your family on a special occasion or to impress your friends with an elegant dinner party. The sauce and stuffing for the squid can be prepared a day in advance, as can the shrimp paste and pumpkin custard. While enjoying dinner, slowly steam the sweet rice that will be served with the custard.

Fried Rice Sticks with Tamarind Sauce (double recipe, page 68)
Mee Krob

Vegetable Soup with Spareribs (page 43)
Tom Jrap-Chai

Spicy Coconut Milk and Chicken Soup (page 35)
Tom Kha Gai

Stuffed Squid in Red Sauce (page 110)
Pla-Mook Sod-Sai Nam-Dang

Chicken in Green Curry (page 77)
Gang Kaeo Wan Gai

Shrimp Paste Sauce (page 28) with Assorted Raw Vegetables
Chilled cabbage leaves, sliced cucumbers and celery hearts
Nam Prik Kapi

Curried Rice (page 49)
Khow Phat Pong Kali

Pumpkin Custard (page 136)
Sung Kha Ya Fuchtong

Sweet Rice (page 137)
Khow Neeow

Thai Dinner for 4 to 6 People

A typical Thai dinner includes one or two soups, one pad or stir-fried dish, one kaeng or gravy/curry dish, and a nam prik served with raw vegetables. I've included a side dish, tapioca balls and a dessert to signify times of prosperity.

Tapioca Balls (page 60)
Saku Sai Mu

Spicy Shrimp Soup (page 37)
Tom Yam Kung

Green Mango and Shrimp Paste Sauce (page 30)
Raw string beans, zucchini slices, cucumber slices and lettuce leaves
Nam Prik Ma Muang

Sesame Chicken with Vegetables (page 75)
Gai Pad Pak

Beef Panang Curry (page 98)
Panang Nuea

Steamed Rice (page 46)
Khow Sook

Sweet Rice Pudding with Longan Fruit (page 138)
Khow Neeow Lum-Yai

Thai-Style Brunch

Next time you serve brunch, make it an unusual and exciting one with these Thai dishes.

To prepare the mango mimosas, fill chilled champagne glasses half full with champagne. Fill the glasses to the top with mango nectar. Garnish with fresh mint leaves.

Mango Mimosas
Thai Salad (page 64)
Salad Kak

Omelette Soup (page 38)
Kaeng Jud Kai

or

Bean Curd Soup with Ground Pork (page 39)
Kaeng Jud Thao Hu

Corn Fritters (page 59)
Khao Pud Tod

Shrimp Fried Rice (page 53)
Khow Pad Koong

Yellow Mung Bean Pudding (page 141)
Thao Suan

Thai Luncheons for 4 People

Thai luncheons are simple affairs, usually including a noodle or fried rice dish and a soup or salad. Desserts or fresh fruit can be served after the meal.

Mixed Salad (page 66)
Yam Yai

Sauteed Noodles in Bean Sauce (page 119)
Pad See-Um

Rice Balls in Coconut Milk (page 140)
Kha Nom Bua-Loi

Pineapple Soup with Pork and Dried Shrimp (page 42)
Kaeng-Jud Sab-Pha-Lot

Dried Shrimp and Shrimp Paste Sauce (page 31)
Raw string beans, cucumber slices, zucchini slices and lettuce leaves
Nam Prik Phao

Crabmeat Fried Rice (page 47)
Khow Pad Puu

Bananas in Coconut Milk (page 144)
Khrow Buad Chi

Thai Cocktail Party for 20 People

Thai food is perfect for large parties where cocktail nibblers and hors d'oeuvres are served. An added advantage is that so many of the dishes may be prepared in advance. For this menu, the turnovers can be made a week in advance and frozen until ready to use. The batters for the fritters and the fish cakes must be prepared a day in advance and refrigerated until frying time. The dried beef can be done several days in advance and stored in a tightly covered container until ready to use. Both desserts can be made a day in advance, too. Serve the dishes on large platters in decorative bowls, garnished with coriander and surrounded by fresh fruits such as mango, pineapple, papaya and oranges.

I've also included an adaptation of a fruit punch my uncle is known for in our village, substituting rice wine for kra-tche, a fermented rice beverage popular in Thailand. I've had great success with this potent, fruity punch. I'm sure you will too.

Uncle Pan's Rice Wine Punch (recipe follows)
Leung Pan Kra-Tche

Curried Chicken Turnovers (double recipe, page 56)
Kha Li Pap Gai

Crabmeat Fritters (page 58)
Nueapu Tod Krob

Lettuce Leaves Stuffed with Shrimp and Coconut (page 67)
Miang Kam

Fish Cakes (page 106)
Tod Man

Dried Beef (page 94)
Nuea Sa-Wan

Shrimp and Shrimp Paste Sauce (page 29)
Nam Prik Kung

Green Mango and Shrimp Paste Sauce (page 30)
Nam Prik Ma Muang

Celery hearts, cucumber slices, string beans, zucchini slices and
chilled steamed cabbage leaves
Mung Bean Pastries (page 134)
Lum Klum

Sweet Rice Cakes Stuffed with Yellow Beans (page 143)
Kha-Nom Tuea Pap

UNCLE PAN'S RICE WINE PUNCH
Leung Pan Kra-tche

2 trays ice cubes
2 teaspoons sugar
½ cup Grand Marnier or other orange liqueur
3 cups bite-size chunks of fresh pineapple
2 cups honeydew and cantaloupe balls
2 cups chilled mango nectar or papaya nectar
1 cup seltzer or club soda
2 quarts rice wine (sake)

Put the ice cubes in a large bowl. Add the sugar and Grand Marnier.
Stir to mix. Add the pineapple, melon balls and nectar. Stir several
times to mix well. Just before serving, gently stir in the seltzer and
rice wine.

Thai Barbecue for 8

Thai food is often prepared on an outdoor grill, called a *thao*, but can be cooked on a barbecue grill just as easily. This meal is perfect for summer entertaining. The sates and Gai Yang are cooked on the grill, and the cucumber salad and bean cake can be prepared ahead of time.

Marinated Beef on Skewers (page 62)
Sate Nuea

Marinated Pork on Skewers (page 62)
Sate Moo

Home-Style Marinated Chicken (double recipe, page 72)
Gai Yang

Cucumber Salad (double recipe, page 65)
Thangua Dong

Steamed Rice (page 46)
Khow Sook

Bean Cake with Coconut Milk (page 139)
Kha Nom Moa-Kang

SOURCE GUIDE

There are many sources for the special items needed in Thai recipes: Thai groceries, Chinese groceries, Spanish markets and health food stores. If you live in an area where these kinds of food stores don't exist, the stores listed below will ship ingredients.

California

Long Beach Market
2009 East Tenth Street
Long Beach, CA 90804
(213) 439–7065

Lynwood Market
11325 Atlantic
Linwood, CA 90202
(213) 635–9457

Illinois

Thai Grocery, Inc.
5014 North Broadway
Chicago, IL 60640
(313) 561–5345

Louisiana

Ho's Market & Parcel Service
1403 West Church Street
Hammond, LA 70401
(504) 542–1666

New York

Poo-Ping
81A Bayard Street
New York, NY 10013
(212) 349–7662

Texas

Thai-Laos Market
9150–A2 South Main Street
Houston, TX 77025
(713) 660–9647

INDEX

appetizers, 55–63
  corn fritters, 59
  crabmeat fritters, 58
  curried chicken turnovers, 56–57
  fried rice sticks with tamarind sauce,
    68–69
  marinated beef on skewers, 62–63
  tapioca balls, 60–61
asparagus soup with crabmeat, 36

bah mi moo dang, 126–127
bai kra prow, 20
bai makrud, 20
bananas in coconut milk, 144
barbecue menu, 152
basil, Oriental, 20
  sauteed chicken with, 79
  sauteed pork with chili peppers and,
    91
basil, seafood with, 104–105
bean cake with coconut milk, 139
bean curd, 15
  soup, with ground pork, 39
beans, *see* mung bean(s); yellow mung
    bean(s)
bean sauce, sauteed noodles in, 119
bean threads, 18
  stir-fried, 128–129
beef, 93–102
  chili, 96
  consomme, yellow noodles with,
    120–121
  dried, 94

fried rice, curried, 51
ginger, 95
  ground, salad, 97
  marinated, on skewers, 62–63
  masaman curry, 99
  in oyster sauce, 102
  panang curry, 98
  in red curry, 101
  salad, 100
  soup, 40
black bean sauce, 17
  capon with, 78–79
black soy sauce, 17
bok choy, 15
bouillabaisse, Thai, 105
broccoli, noodles with shrimp and,
    130–131
broth, Thai chicken, 34
brunch menu, 148

cabbage, Chinese, 15
cakes:
  bean, with coconut milk, 139
  chicken, 76–77
  fish, 106–107
  sweet rice, stuffed with yellow beans,
    143
capon with black bean sauce, 78–79
cayenne pepper, 19
chicken, 71–79
  broth, Thai, 34
  cakes, 76–77

and chicken livers, in red curry sauce, 74

and coconut milk soup, spicy, 35

in green curry, 77

legs, baked in red sauce, 82

marinated, 72–73

sauteed, with Oriental basil, 79

sesame, with vegetables, 75

soup, Thai, noodles with, 124–125

turnovers, curried, 56–57

chili beef, 96

chili peppers, 18–19

green, in fish sauce, 32

pork fried rice with, 52

sauteed pork with basil and, 91

Chinese cabbage, 15

cocktail party menu, 150–151

coconut, lettuce leaves stuffed with shrimp and, 67–68

coconut milk, 15

bananas in, 144

bean cake with, 139

and chicken soup, spicy, 35

peanut dipping sauce, 63

peanut salad dressing, 64–65

rice balls in, 140

condiments, 50

see also dipping pastes and sauces

coriander, 19

corn fritters, 59

crabmeat:

asparagus soup with, 36

fried rice, 47

fritters, 58

crushed red pepper, 19

cucumber salad, 65

curries:

beef fried rice, 51

beef masaman, 99

beef panang, 98

chicken turnovers, 56–57

green, chicken in, 77

pork and watercress in, 86–87

rice, 49

shrimp with pineapple, 111

see also red curry

curry pastes, 21–26

green, 25

masaman, 23

panang, 24

red, 22

sour, 24–25

yellow, 26

curry powder, 19

custards:

pumpkin, 136

Thai, 135

dat chan taet, 20

desserts, 133–144

bananas in coconut milk, 144

bean cake with coconut milk, 139

mung bean pastries, 134

mung beans with brown sugar, 142

pumpkin custard, 136

rice balls in coconut milk, 140

sweet rice, 137

sweet rice cakes stuffed with yellow beans, 143

sweet rice pudding with longan fruit, 138

Thai custard, 135

yellow mung bean pudding, 141

dinner menus, 146–147

dipping pastes and sauces, 27–32, 72–73, 107

dried shrimp and shrimp paste, 31

green chili peppers in fish sauce, 32

green mango and shrimp paste, 30

peanut-coconut, 63

shrimp and shrimp paste, 29

shrimp paste, 28

dried beef, 94

dried shrimp, *see* shrimp, dried

duck with preserved lemon, 80–81

egg:

omelette soup, 38

spinach soup with, 41

equipment, 14–15

fish:
  cakes, 106–107
  deep-fried, in spicy-sweet sauce, 108
  deep-fried, in tangy ginger sauce, 109
  in red curry, 113
  steamed, 115
  stew, ginger, 114
  see also crabmeat; seafood; shrimp
fish sauce, 17
  green chili peppers in, 32
five-spice powder, 19
fried rice, 46
  beef, curried, 51
  crabmeat, 47
  pineapple, 48–49
  pork, with chili peppers, 52
  shrimp, 53
  shrimp paste, 50–51
  sticks with tamarind sauce, 68–69
fritters, 58–59
  corn, 59
  crabmeat, 58

gai, 71–79, 82
gai pad bai kra prow, 79
gai pad pak, 75
gai-thong tow tchiow, 78–79
gai yang, 72–73
galanga root, 19–20
gang gai, 74
gang kaeo wan gai, 77
gang som, 112–113
garlic, 20
ginger, 20
  beef, 95
  fish stew, 114
  ground pork with, 85
  sauce, tangy, deep-fried fish in, 109
green chili peppers in fish sauce, 32
green curry paste, 25
green mango and shrimp paste sauce, 30

hed, 16
herbs, 18–20

herb sauce, pork in, 88
homok tat-le, 104–105
hua chai po, 16

ingredients, 13, 15–20
  basic, 15–17
  herbs and spices, 18–20
  noodles, 18
  sauces, 17
  source guide for, 153

kaeng jud, 33
kaeng-jud hed-nu, 44
kaeng jud kai, 38
kaeng jud phak khom, 41
kaeng-jud-sab-pha-lot, 42
kaeng jud thao hu, 39
kaeng-khow sapbhalot, 111
kaeng nuea, 101
kang moo te-po, 86–87
kapi, 16
ka-ti, 15
kha, 19–20
kha-gai oeb nam-dang, 82
kha li pap gai, 56–57
kha-nom, 133–144
kha nom bua-loi, 140
kha nom moa-kang, 139
kha-nom tuea pap, 143
khao pud tod, 59
khing, 20
khong wang, 55–63, 68–69
khow, 16, 45–53
khow krook kapi, 50–51
khow moo pad prik, 52
khow neeow, 16, 137
khow neeow lum-yai, 138
khow pad, 46
khow pad koong, 53
khow pad nam prik kang nuea, 51
khow pad puu, 47
khow pat prik sapbhalot, 48–49
khow phat pong kali, 49
khow sook, 46

khrok, 14
kra dook moo tod, 89
kra thiam, 20
kuwae tee-ow, 117–132
kuwae tee-ow gai, 124–125
kuwae tee-ow nuea, 120–121

lap nuea, 97
lemon, preserved, duck with, 80–81
lemon grass, 20
lettuce leaves stuffed with shrimp and
    coconut, 67–68
Leung Pan kra-tche, 151
light soy sauce, 17
lime, makrud, 20
longan fruit, sweet rice pudding with,
    138
lum klum, 134
luncheon menus, 149

mace, 20
mai fun pad moo, 132
ma kham, 16
makrud lime, 20
mango, green, and shrimp paste sauce,
    30
masaman curry:
    beef, 99
    paste, 23
masaman nuea, 99
mee krob, 68–69
menus, 145–152
    barbecue for 8, 152
    brunch, 148
    cocktail party for 20 people, 150–151
    dinner for 4 to 6 people, 147
    feast for 6 to 8 people, 146
    luncheons for 4 people, 149
miang kam, 67–68
mixed salad, 66–67
moo, 83–92
moo dang, 90
moo pad bai kra pow, 91
moo pad kapi, 87

moo pad preaw wan, 84
moo pad prik keeng, 92
moo pad woon sen, 129
moo pa-ro, 88
moo wan, 86
mung bean(s):
    with brown sugar, 142
    pastries, 134
    see also yellow mung bean(s)
mushrooms, straw, 16

nam jim gai yang, 72–73
nam jim sate, 63
nam man hoi, 17
nam-man put, 17
nam pla, 17, 107
nam pla prik pboen, 32
nam prik, 27–32
nam prik kaeng, 21–26
nam prik kaeng dang, 22
nam prik kaeng khali, 26
nam prik kaeng kheu wan, 25
nam prik kaeng masaman, 23
nam prik kaeng panang, 24
nam prik kaeng sum, 24–25
nam prik kapi, 28
nam prik kung, 29
nam prik ma muang, 30
nam prik phao, 31
nam salad kak, 64–65
nam sod, 85
nam thaan bip, 15
noodles, 18, 117–132
    rice, sauteed, 122–123
    rice flakes with pork, 118
    rice vermicelli sauteed with pork, 132
    sauteed, in bean sauce, 119
    with shrimp and broccoli, 130–131
    stir-fried bean threads, 128–129
    with Thai chicken soup, 124–125
    yellow, with beef consomme, 120–121
    yellow, with roast pork, 126–127
nuea, 93–102
nuea nom thok, 100

nuea pad keeng, 95
nuea pad pak nam-mon hoi, 102
nuea pad prik, 96
nueapu tod krob, 58
nuea sa-wan, 94

oil, vegetable, 17
omelette soup, 38
oyster sauce, 17
   beef in, 102

pad lad-na kung, 130–131
pad see-um, 119
pad thai, 122–123
pad woon sen, 128–129
pak chee, 19
palm sugar, 15
panang curry:
   beef, 98
   paste, 24
panang nuea, 98
pastries, mung bean, 134
peanut(s), 15
   coconut milk dipping sauce, 63
   coconut milk salad dressing, 64–65
phao pad woon sen, 129
phed tun ma-nao dong, 80–81
pickled turnips, 16
pineapple:
   curried shrimp with, 111
   fried rice, 48–49
   soup, with pork and dried shrimp, 42
pla gian, 109
pla lad prik, 108
pla-mook sod-sai nam-dang, 110–111
pla nuang, 115
pong kha-li, 19
pong pa-lo, 19
pork, 83–92
   fried rice with chili peppers, 52
   ground, bean curd soup with, 39
   ground, tree fungus soup with, 44
   ground, with ginger, 85
   in herb sauce, 88

pineapple soup with dried shrimp
   and, 42
rice flakes with, 118
rice vermicelli sauteed with, 132
roast, with red gravy, 90
roast, yellow noodles with, 126–127
sauteed, with basil and chili peppers,
   91
sauteed, with red curry, 92
sauteed, with shrimp paste, 87
sauteed spareribs with onions and
   pepper, 89
stir-fried bean threads with, 129
sweet, 86
sweet and sour, 84
and watercress in curry, 86–87
po-tak, 105
prik, 18–19
prik pboen, 19
puddings:
   sweet rice, with longan fruit, 138
   yellow mung bean, 141
pumpkin custard, 136

red curry:
   beef in, 101
   chicken and chicken livers in, 74
   fish in, 113
   paste, 22
   sauteed pork with, 92
red pepper, crushed, 19
red sauce:
   baked chicken legs in, 82
   stuffed squid in, 110–111
rice, 16, 45–53
   balls, in coconut milk, 140
   cakes, sweet, stuffed with yellow
      beans, 143
   curried, 49
   pudding, sweet, with longan fruit, 138
   steamed, 46
   sticky, 16
   sweet, 137
   see also fried rice

rice flakes, 18
  with pork, 118
rice noodles, 18
  sauteed, 122–123
rice vermicelli, 18
  sauteed with pork, 132
rice wine punch, Uncle Pan's, 151

saku, 16
saku sai mu, 60–61
salad dressing, peanut-coconut milk,
    64–65
salad kak, 64–65
salads, 55, 64–68
  beef, 100
  cucumber, 65
  ground beef, 97
  lettuce leaves stuffed with shrimp and
    coconut, 67–68
  mixed, 66–67
  Thai, 64–65
salut, 55, 64–68
sate nuea, 62–63
sauces, 17
  see also dipping pastes and sauces
seafood, 103–115
  with basil, 104–105
  stuffed squid in red sauce, 110–111
  Thai bouillabaisse, 105
  see also crabmeat; fish; shrimp
see u dam, 17
see u kow, 17
sen, 18, 117–132
sen kuwae chap, 18
sen kuwae-chap pad moo, 118
sen lek, 18
sen mee, 18
serving of Thai meal, 11–12
sesame chicken with vegetables, 75
shrimp:
  curried, with pineapple, 111
  fried rice, 53
  noodles with broccoli and, 130–131
  and shrimp paste sauce, 29

soup, spicy, 37
stew, spicy sour, 112–113
shrimp, dried:
  lettuce leaves stuffed with coconut
    and, 67–68
  pineapple soup with pork and, 42
  and shrimp paste sauce, 31
  stir-fried bean threads with, 129
shrimp paste, 16
  and dried shrimp sauce, 31
  fried rice, 50–51
  and green mango sauce, 30
  sauce, 28
  sauteed pork with, 87
  and shrimp sauce, 29
shu-shi pla, 113
soup, 33
soup gai, 34
soup naw mai, 36
soup nuea, 40
soups, 33–44
  asparagus, with crabmeat, 36
  bean curd, with ground pork, 39
  beef, 40
  chicken, noodles with, 124–125
  omelette, 38
  pineapple, with pork and dried
    shrimp, 42
  spicy coconut milk and chicken, 35
  spicy shrimp, 37
  spinach, with egg, 41
  Thai chicken broth, 34
  tree fungus, with ground pork, 44
  vegetable, with spareribs, 43
sour curry paste, 24–25
soy sauce, 17
spareribs:
  sauteed, with onions and pepper, 89
  vegetable soup with, 43
spices, 18–20
spicy:
  coconut milk and chicken soup, 35
  shrimp soup, 37
  sour shrimp stew, 112–113
  sweet sauce, deep-fried fish in, 108

spinach soup with egg, 41
squid, stuffed, in red sauce, 110–111
steamers, 14–15
stews:
   ginger fish, 114
   spicy sour shrimp, 112–113
sticky rice, 16
straw mushrooms, 16
sung kha ya, 135
sung kha ya fuchtong, 136
sweet:
   pork, 86
   rice, 137
   rice cakes stuffed with yellow beans,
     143
   rice pudding with longan fruit, 138
   and sour pork, 84

ta krai, 20
tamarind, 16
   sauce, fried rice sticks with, 68–69
tapioca, 16
   balls, 60–61
tat-le, 103–115
thangua dong, 65
thao hu, 15
thao suan, 141
tod krob, 58–59
tod man, 106–107
tod man gai, 76–77
tom jrap-chai, 43
tom kha gai, 35

tom som, 114
tom yam, 33
tom yam kung, 37
tow tchiow, 17
tree fungus soup with ground pork, 44
tua, 15
tuea-keow tom nam-tan, 142
turnips, pickled, 16
turnovers, curried chicken, 56–57

Uncle Pan's rice wine punch, 151

vegetable soup with spareribs, 43
vegetable oil, 17

watercress and pork in curry, 86–87
woks, 14
woon sen, 18

yam yai, 66–67
yellow curry paste, 26
yellow mung bean(s):
   cake, with coconut milk, 139
   pudding, 141
   sweet rice cakes stuffed with, 143
yellow noodles:
   with beef consomme, 120–121
   with roast pork, 126–127